INSIGHT GUIDES

JAPANESE

PHRASEBOOK & DICTIONARY

D0172401

Contacting the Editors

Every effort has been made to provide accurate information in this publication, but changes are inevitable. The publisher cannot be responsible for any resulting loss, inconvenience or injury. We would appreciate it if readers would call our attention to any errors or outdated information. We also welcome your suggestions; if you come across a relevant expression not in our phrase book, please contact us at: hello@insightguides.com

All Rights Reserved
© 2015 APA Publications (UK) Ltd.

First Edition: 2015
Printed in China

Cover & Interior Design: Pawel Pasternak
Production: AM Services
Production Manager: Vicky Glover
Picture Researcher: Slawek Krajewski
Cover Photo: all iStockphoto

Interior Photos: all iStockphoto

CONTENTS

FOOD & DRINK

GOING OUT

DICTIONARY

PRONUNCIATION

This section is designed to familiarize you with the sounds of Japanese using simplified phonetic transcription. The pronunciation of the Japanese sounds is explained below, together with their 'imitated' equivalents. This system is used throughout the phrase book. When you see a word spelled phonetically, simply read the pronunciation as if it were English, noting any special rules.

Japanese is a unique language. Apart from a similarity of script (the Japanese adopted Chinese ideograms) it bears no resemblance to Chinese or other Asian languages, except for Korean. Where Japanese comes from is still a matter of conjecture. Japan, its people, customs, and language were almost totally isolated until the late nineteenth century.

Today there are many foreign 'loan' words that have been adopted into Japanese. From **pan** (from the Portuguese for bread) to **sportsman**, you will come across many foreign words, the majority of which are from English. At first hearing, you may not recognize these words because of the change in pronunciation and, conversely, you may not be understood when using a 'loan' word until you give it a Japanese pronunciation.

Japanese is composed less of vowels and consonants than of syllables, consisting of a consonant and a vowel. Consonants are always followed by vowels, except for **n**, which can occur alone. All syllables are pronounced with equal force: there is no stress except for emphasis.

CONSONANTS

Letter	Approximate Pronunciation	Symbol	Example	Pronunciation
b	approximately as in English	**b**	バス	*basu*
ch	approximately as in English	**ch**	お茶	*ocha*

Letter	Approximate Pronunciation	Symbol	Example	Pronunciation
d	approximately as in English	d	電車	*densha*
g	approximately as in English	d	外国	*gaikoku*
h	approximately as in English	h	箱根	*hakone*
j	approximately as in English	j	原宿	*harajuku*
k	approximately as in English	k	観光	*kankoo*
m	approximately as in English	m	鎌倉	*kamakura*
p	approximately as in English	p	乾杯	*kanpai*
s	approximately as in English	s	寿司	*sushi*
t	approximately as in English	t	成田	*narita*

Letter	Approximate Pronunciation	Symbol	Example	Pronunciation
f	with lips flattened and without putting lower teeth against lower lip, between an f and an h	f	お風呂	*ofuro*
n	1. before vowels like n in now	n	長い	*nagai*
	2. at the end of a word, said without letting your tongue touch the roof of your mouth	n	さん	*san*

r	with tip of tongue against the gum behind the upper front teeth, between an r and an 1	r	りんご	*ringo*
w [semi-vowel]	the lips are not rounded but left slack	w	分かる	*wakaru*

Letter	Approximate Pronunciation	Symbol	Example	Pronunciation
z	1. at the beginning of words, like ds in beds	z	ゼロ	*zero*
	2. In the middle of words like z in zoo	z	水	*mizu*

Double consonants should be pronounced 'long', i.e. hold the sound for a moment. The doubling of a consonant is important as it can change the meaning of a word.

kk	一個	*ikko*
pp	かっぱ	*kappa*
tt	ちょっと	*chotto*

VOWELS

Letter	Approximate Pronunciation	Symbol	Example	Pronunciation
A	like the a in father, Pronounced forward in the mouth	a	魚	*sakana*
e	like e in get	e	テレビ	*terebi*
i	like i in sit	i	イギリス	*igirisu*
o	like o in note	o	男	*otoko*
u	like u in put, but without rounding the lips	u	冬	*fuyu*

Long vowels (**aa**, **ee**, **ii**, **oo**, **uu**) are held for twice the amount of time. This is important in Japanese and can change the meaning of words, e.g. **oba(san)** means aunt while **obaa(san)** means grandmother.

Vowel clusters: when two vowels occur together (**ie, ai, ue, ao**) they should be pronounced separately with each vowel keeping its normal sound.

Consonant/double vowel clusters: (e.g. **kya, kyu, kyo**) these are two sounds said quickly so that they become one: **kya** is **ki** and **ya**.

Whispered vowels: sometimes **i** and **u** are devoiced, that is whispered or even omitted. This happens when **i** and **u** occur at the end of a word, or between voiceless consonants: **ch, f, h, k, p, s, sh, t,** and **ts**.

Japanese is composed of three different 'scripts' or ways of writing: **kanji** (Chinese characters or ideograms), **hiragana** (an alphabet in which each symbol represents a spoken syllable), and **katakana** (another alphabet). These three systems are used in combination to write modern Japanese.

Hiragana is used to link **kanji** characters together.

Katakana is used to write foreign 'loan' words, most of which are English in origin.

In addition to these three 'scripts' you will find **romaji**, the Romanized system used to write Japanese. In Japan important signs and names are often given in **romaji**, for example the names of subway stations.

Traditionally Japanese is written from the top to the bottom of the page starting in the upper right-hand corner. Today it is also commonly written horizontally and from left to right. The Japanese phrases you will see in this book incorporate a mixture of **kanji**, **hiragana** and **katakana**, and the pronunciation is in **romaji**. Japanese words and phrases are pronounced very evenly, and stress is used only to emphasize meaning. Pitch does vary however; normal sentences will begin on a high note and finish on a low note.

As in English, questions normally rise in pitch at the end of the sentence.

HOW TO USE THE APP

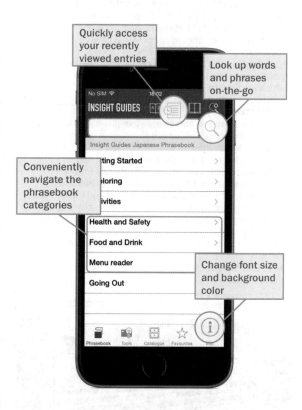

Quickly access your recently viewed entries

Look up words and phrases on-the-go

Conveniently navigate the phrasebook categories

Change font size and background color

Save the most useful everyday words and phrases to your Favorites

Use the Flash Cards Quiz to learn and memorize new words easily

Take all digital advantages of the app: listen to words and phrases pronounced by native speakers

No SIM 🗢   18:16

Insight Guides Japanese Phrasebook

Is there a traditional Japanese/ inexpensive restaurant nearby?

この近くに料亭 /
安いレストラン は   すか。

*kono chikaku ni ryootei /
yasui resutoran waarimasu ka*

Can you reco...   A table for......

Phrasebook   Tools   Catalogue   Favourites   Info

To learn how to activate the app, see the inside back cover of this phrasebook.

THE BASICS

GRAMMAR

REGULAR VERBS

At first glance Japanese verbs are very straightforward, with only present and past tenses and no special form to indicate person or number. Future tense is gauged from the context. However, verbs are subject to other changes to express variety of degrees of politeness and mood. The two basic verb forms are:

taberu	to eat	**nomu**	to drink
tabemasu	to eat	**nomimasu**	to drink
(polite form)		(polite form)	

This phrase book uses the polite form throughout.

tabemasu	(I, you, he, she, we, they) eat
tabemasen	(I, you, he, she, we, they) don't/doesn't eat
tabemashita	(I, you, he, she, we, they) ate
tabemasendeshita	(I, you, he, she, we, they) didn't eat

In addition to the above forms, verbs can indicate such functions as causative, command, conditional, passive, potential etc. by adding appropriate suffixes. For example:

tabesasemasu	I cause (someone) to eat
tabero!	Eat!
tabereba	if you eat...

PARTICLES

Japanese uses a number of particles to mark the use, or add to the meaning of the word they follow in a sentence.

ga	subject marker	**nodo ga itai desu**	literal meaning: The throat is sore.

wa	attention-directing marker	**watashi wa nodo ga itai desu**	literal meaning: As for me the throat is sore.
o	object marker	**gohan o tabemasu**	literal meaning: I eat rice.

IRREGULAR VERBS

Japanese has only two irregular verbs: **suru** (to do) and **kuru** (to come). Their polite forms are as follows:

shimasu	do	**kimasu**	come
shimasen	don't/ doesn't do	**kimasen**	don't/ doesn't come
shimashita	did	**kimashita**	came
shimasendeshita	didn't do	**kimasendeshita**	didn't come

NOUNS & ARTICLES

Japanese nouns have no articles, and no plurals. All nouns have one single form that does not change according to the noun's role in a sentence.

Personal pronouns are used sparingly in Japanese. Use the person's name + **san** instead of a pronoun, or omit the pronoun completely if it is clear who is being addressed or referred to. Personal pronouns are:

watashib	I	**anata*** (singular)	you
watashi tachi	we	**anatagata*** (plural)	you

* These pronouns are very familiar and appropriate only between husband and wife or boyfriend and girlfriend.

WORD ORDER

Japanese questions are formed by adding the particle **ka** (a verbal question mark) to the verb at the end of a sentence. Note that in Japanese the verb always comes last. The basic rule for word order within a sentence is: subject – object – verb

Watashi wa Smith desu.   I'm (Mr./Mrs.) Smith.
Honda-san* desu ka?   Are you (Mr./Mrs.) Honda?
*When addressing a Japanese person you should use the family name followed by san. (Do not use san when referring to yourself!)

IMPERATIVES

There are many ways to indicate an order, depending on how strong you would like it to be. Following is an example of imperative from mild to strong:

Go!   **Itte**   **Ikinasai**   **Ike**

COMPARATIVE & SUPERLATIVE

Unlike English, Japanese adjectives do not indicate comparative or superlative. Instead Japanese employs the following pattern:

Comparative: A **to** B **to dochira ga** adjective **desuka?**
Tookyoo to Oosaka to dochira ga ookii desu ka.
Which is bigger, Tokyo or Osaka?

Superlative: A **to** B **to** C **de** A **ga ichiban** adjective **desu.**
Tookyoo to Oosaka to Kyooto de Tookyoo ga ichiban ookii desu.
Among Tokyo, Osaka and Kyoto, Tokyo is the biggest.

POSSESSIVE PRONOUNS

To make possessive pronouns, use the grammar marker **no** following the person's name or the personal pronoun.

Honda-san no hon   Mr./Mrs. Honda's book
Watashi no hon   my book

ADJECTIVES

A Japanese adjective ends in **i** and modifies a noun that is placed immediately after it. For example, 'a big room' will be **ookii** heya. Japanese adjectives are very different from their English counter parts, and behave more like verbs. The past tense of most adjectives is formed by adding **-katta** to the basic stem:

takai	expensive	**yasui**	cheap
takakatta	(was) expensive	**yasukatta**	(was) cheap

There is another group of adjectives that takes **na** at the end of the word to modify a noun.

Example: **kiree-na hana** (pretty flower), **taisetsu-na mono** (an important thing), **shizuka-na tokoro** (a quiet place).

ADVERBS

An adverb describes a verb. Many Japanese adverbs end in **ku**, and are derived from adjectives by replacing the final **i** of an adjective with **ku**.

Example: **Hayaku hashirimashita.** He ran quickly.

GETTING STARTED

THE BASICS

NUMBERS

NEED TO KNOW

0	零/ゼロ
	ree/zero
1	一
	ichi
2	二
	ni
3	三
	san
4	四
	shi/yon
5	五
	go
6	六
	roku
7	七
	shichi/nana
8	八
	hachi
9	九
	kyuu/ku
10	十
	juu
11	十一
	juuichi
12	十二
	juuni

13	十三
	juusan
14	十四
	juushi/juuyon
15	十五
	juugo
16	十六
	juuroku
17	十七
	juushichi/juunana
18	十八
	juuhachi
19	十九
	juukyuu/juuku
20	二十
	nijuu
21	二十一
	nijuuichi
22	二十二
	nijuuni
30	三十
	sanjuu
31	三十一
	sanjuuichi
40	四十
	yonjuu/shijuu
50	五十
	gojuu
60	六十
	rokujuu
70	七十
	nanajuu/shichijuu

80	八十	
	hachijuu	
90	九十	
	kyuujuu	
100	百	
	hyaku	
101	百一	
	hyakuichi	
200	二百	
	nihyaku	
500	五百	
	gohyaku	
1,000	千	
	sen	
10,000	一万	
	ichiman	
1,000,000	百万	
	hyakuman	

ORDINAL NUMBERS

first	一番	
	ichiban	
second	二番	
	niban	
third	三番	
	sanban	
fourth	四番	
	yonban	
fifth	五番	
	goban	

once	一回
	ikkai
twice	二回
	nikai
three times	三回
	sankai

(i)

In Japanese, there are two ways of counting to ten. There are general numbers (listed on page 20) used for talking about sums of money, telephone numbers, etc. There is also a system for combining a number with an object-specific counter. This system groups objects into types according to shape and size. There are specific ways of counting flat objects, animals, people, etc. Luckily the counter system only applies to numbers from 1–10. After 10 the general number is used. When you are not sure of the correct counter, you can always use the 'all-purpose' counters listed below.

ALL PURPOSE COUNTERS (NUMBERS 1–10)

These counters are strictly used to count 'unclassifiable' objects (objects where shape or size are difficult to determine). When you don't know the specific counter use:

1	**hitotsu**	2	**futatsu**
3	**mittsu**	4	**yottsu**
5	**itsutsu**	6	**muttsu**
7	**nanatsu**	8	**yattsu**
9	**kokonotsu**	10	**too**

OTHER COUNTERS

Flat objects (stamps, paper, etc.)

1	**ichimai**	6	**rokumai**
2	**nimai**	7	**nanamai/ shichimai**
3	**sanmai**	8	**hachimai**
4	**yonmai**	9	**kyuumai**
5	**gomai**	10	**juumai**

People

1	**hitori**	6	**rokunin**
2	**futari**	7	**nananin/ shichinin**
3	**sannin**	8	**hachinin**
4	**yonin**	9	**kyuunin**
5	**gonin**	10	**juunin**

Long, thin objects (pen, bottle, umbrella, etc.)

1	**ippon**	6	**roppon**
2	**nihon**	7	**nanahon**
3	**sanbon**	8	**happon**
4	**yonhon**	9	**kyuuhon**
5	**gohon**	10	**juppon**

For example, the counter for a bottle is **nihon**.

I'd like two bottles of beer.   **Biru o nihon kudasai.**

If you didn't know the counter, you could use the 'all-purpose' counter:

I'd like two bottles of beer.   **Biiru o futatsu kudasai.**

Note that the counter usually follows the word it qualifies.

TIME

NEED TO KNOW

What time is it?	何時ですか。
	nanji desu ka
It's noon [midday].	十二時（正午）です。
	juuniji (shoogo) desu
At midnight.	真夜中に
	mayonaka ni
From nine o'clock to	九時から五時まで
	kuji kara goji made
5 o'clock.	
Twenty [after] past	四時二十分
	yoji nijuppun
four	
A quarter to nine	九時十五分前
	kuji juugorun mae
5:30 a.m./p.m.	午前/午後五時三十分
	gozen/gogo goji sanjuppun

In ordinary conversation, time is expressed as shown above. For airline and train timetables, however, the 24-hour clock is used.
Japan is nine hours ahead of GMT all year round. Japan does not change its clocks to reflect winter and summer time.

DAYS

NEED TO KNOW

Sunday	日曜日 *nichiyoobi*
Monday	月曜日 *getsuyoobi*
Tuesday	火曜日 *kayoobi*
Wednesday	水曜日 *suiyoobi*
Thursday	木曜日 *mokuyoobi*
Friday	金曜日 *kinyoobi*
Saturday	土曜日 *doyoobi*

Japan changed from lunar calendar to the Gregorian calendar in 1873. However, the lunar calendar is still used in farming, and in other activities in rural areas of Japan. Japanese calendars start with Sunday and end with Saturday.

DATES

yesterday	昨日 *kinoo*

today	今日
	kyoo
tomorrow	明日
	ashita
day	日
	nichi/hi
week	週
	shuu
month	月
	tsuki
year	年
	toshi

> (i)
>
> Dates in Japan are written in Year-Month-Day format. January 1st, 2010 would be 2010 年1月1日 **nisen juu nen ichi gatsu tsuitachi**, or 2010, January, first.

MONTHS

January	一月
	ichigatsu
February	二月
	nigatsu
March	三月
	sangatsu
April	四月
	shigatsu
May	五月
	gogatsu
June	六月
	rokugatsu

July	七月
	shichigatsu
August	八月
	hachigatsu
September	九月
	kugatsu
October	十月
	juugatsu
November	十一月
	juuichigatsu
December	十二月
	juunigatsu

SEASONS

the spring	春
	haru
the summer	夏
	natsu
the fall [autumn]	秋
	aki
the winter	冬
	fuyu

HOLIDAYS

Public holidays
January 1 **ganjitsu/gantan** New Year's Day
Second Monday in January **seejin no hi** Adult's Day
February 11 **kenkoku kinen no hi** National Foundation Day
March 21* **shunbun no hi** Vernal Equinox Day
April 29 **midori no hi** Greenery Day
May 3 **kenpoo kinen bi** Constitution Day
May 5 **kodomo no hi** Children's Day
September 15 **keeroo no hi** Respect for the Aged Day
September 23* **shuubun no hi** Autumnal Equinox Day
October 10 **taiiku no hi** Health-Sports Day
November 3 **bunka no hi** Culture Day
November 23 **kinroo kansha no hi** Labor Thanksgiving Day
December 23 **tennoo tanjoobi** Emperor's Birthday
* These dates are lunar and change year by year.

The most important holiday in Japan is New Year's day. All the stores are closed on the January first, and some will close on the second and third as well. Adult's Day (second Monday in January) is designated to celebrate those who are and will be 20 during the year. The week from Greenery Day (April 29) to Children's Day (May 5) is called the Golden Week. Many people take advantage of the four holidays falling during this week (Greenery Day, May Day, Constitution Day, and Children's Day) to travel, thus creating traffic jams everywhere. Bon Festival, from August 13 to 16, is a time when many people go to their ancestral home: the souls of the deceased ancestors are considered to come home during this time.

ARRIVAL & DEPARTURE

NEED TO KNOW

I'm here on vacation [holiday]/business.	観光/仕事で来ました。
	kankoo/shigoto de kimashita
I'm going to...	...へ行きます。
	...e ikimasu
I'm staying at the... Hotel.	...ホテルに泊まっています。
	...hoteru ni tomatte imasu

YOU MAY HEAR...

チケット/パスポートをお見せください。 *chiketto/pasupooto o omise kudasai*	Your ticket/ passport, please.
今回の旅行の目的は何ですか。 *konkai no ryokoo no mokuteki wa nan desu ka*	What's the purpose of your visit?
どこにお泊まりですか。 *doko ni otomari desu ka*	Where are you staying?
後、どのくらいいらっしゃいますか。 *ato donokurai irasshaimasu ka*	How long are you staying?
どなたとご一緒ですか。 *donata to goissho desu ka*	Who are you with?

BORDER CONTROL

I'm just passing through.	立ち寄るだけです。
	tachiyoru dake desu

MONEY

NEED TO KNOW

Where's...?	...はどこですか。
	...wa doko desu ka
the ATM	キャッシュコーナー
	kyasshu koonaa
the bank	銀行
	ginkoo
the currency	両替所
exchange office	*ryoogaejo*
What time does the bank open/close?	銀行は何時から/までですか。
	ginkoo wa nanji kara/made desu ka
I'd like to change dollars/pounds to yen	ドル/ポンドを円に替えたいんですが。
	doru/pondo o en ni kaetain desu ga
I want to cash some traveler's checks [cheques].	トラベラーズチェックを換金したいんですが。
	toraberaazu chekku o kankin shitain desu ga

I would like to declare...	…を申告します。 *...o shinkoku shimasu*
I have nothing to declare.	申告するものはありません。 *shinkoku suru mono wa arimasen*

YOU MAY HEAR...

申告するものはありますか。
shinkoku suru mono wa arimasu ka

Do you have anything to declare?

関税がかかります。
kanzee ga kakarimasu

You must pay duty on this.

このバッグを開けてください。
kono baggu o akete kudasai

Please open this bag.

YOU MAY SEE...

税関検査 *zeekan kensa*	customs
免税品 *menzeehin*	duty-free goods
課税 *kazee*	goods to declare
免税 *menzee*	nothing to declare
入国手続き *nyuukoku tetsuzuki*	passport control
警察 *keesatsu*	police

YOU MAY SEE...

カードを入れる	insert card
キャンセルする	cancel
消去する	clear
入力する	enter
暗証番号	PIN
引き出す	withdraw funds
当座預金口座から	from checking [current] account
普通預金口座から	from savings account
レシート/領収書	receipt

AT THE BANK

Can I exchange foreign currency here?	外国通貨の両替はできますか。 *gaikoku tsuuka no ryoogae wa dekimasu ka*
What's the exchange rate?	為替レートはいくらですか。 *kawase reeto wa ikura desu ka*
How much is the fee?	手数料はいくらですか。 *tesuuryoo wa ikura desu ka*
I've lost my traveler's checks [cheques].	トラベラーズチェックをなくしました。 *toraberaazu chekku o nakushimashita*
My card was lost.	カードをなくしました。 *kaado o nakushimashita*
My credit cards have been stolen.	クレジットカードを盗まれました。 *kurejitto kaado o nusumaremashita*
My card doesn't work.	カードが使えません。 *kaado ga tsukaemasen*

YOU MAY SEE...

The monetary system is the yen (円), abbreviated to ¥.
Coins: ¥1, ¥5, ¥10, ¥50, ¥100, and ¥500
Notes: ¥1,000, ¥2,000, ¥5,000, and ¥10,000

Banks are open from 9:00 a.m. to 5:00 p.m.
Monday through Friday. Some banks are open on
Saturdays and all banks are closed on Sundays, except the
bank at Tokyo Airport, which is open 24 hours a day.
Most banks have a foreign currency section. You will
need to show your passport to change foreign currency or
traveler's checks. You will usually be invited to sit down
while the transaction is conducted, which may take as long
as 15 minutes. Your name will be called when your money
is ready.
You will not be able to use foreign credit cards to get cash
from most ATMs, except those run by Citibank and the
Japan Post Bank postal service. Every post office in Japan
has an ATM where you can obtain cash using international
credit cards or cash cards from your bank. In rural areas,
note that banks may not have currency exchange facilities
at all so the safest solution is to have cash with you at all
times.

CONVERSATION

NEED TO KNOW

Hello.	こんにちは。 *konnichiwa*
How are you?	お元気ですか。 *ogenki desu ka*
Fine, thanks.	はい、おかげさまで。 *hai okage sama de*
Excuse me! (to get attention)	失礼します。 *shitsuree shimasu*
Do you speak English?	英語ができますか。 *eego ga dekimasu ka*
What's your name?	お名前は。 *onamae wa*
My name is…	…です。 *…desu*
Pleased to meet you.	よろしくお願いします。 *yoroshiku onegai shimasu*
Where are you from?	どちらからですか。 *dochira kara desu ka*

I'm from the U.S./U.K.	アメリカ/イギリスからです。
	amerika/igirisu kara desu
What do you do?	何をしていますか。
	nani o shite imasu ka
I work for...	…に勤めています。
	...ni tsutomete imasu
I'm a student.	学生です。
	gakusee desu
I'm retired.	退職しました。
	taishoku shimashita
Do you like...?	は好きですか。
	...wa suki desu ka
Goodbye.	さようなら。
	sayoonara
See you later.	それではまた。
	sore dewa mata

LANGUAGE DIFFICULTIES

Do you speak English?	英語ができますか
	eego ga dekimasu ka
Does anyone here speak English?	英語ができる人はいますか。
	eego ga dekiru hito wa imasu ka
I don't speak (much) Japanese.	(あまり)日本語ができません。
	(amari) nihongo ga dekimasen
Could you speak more slowly?	ゆっくり言ってくれませんか。
	yukkuri itte kuremasen ka
Could you repeat that?	もう一度、言ってくれませんか。
	moo ichido itte kuremasen ka
Excuse me? [Pardon?]	すみません
	sumimasen

What was that?	何ですか。 *nan desu ka*
Please write it down.	書いてください。 *kaite kudasai*
Can you translate this for me?	訳してください。 *yakushite kudasai*
What does this/that mean?	これ/それは、何という意味ですか。 *kore/sore wa nan to yuu imi desu ka*
I understand.	分力、りました。 *wakarimashita*
I don't understand.	分かりません。 *wakarimasen*
Do you understand?	分力、り ます力、。 *wakarimasu ka*

> (i)
>
> It is customary in Japan to address people by their last name first, though more recently when meeting foreigners many Japanese will give their surname last. Generally, the suffix-**san** (Mr., Mrs., or Ms.) is used after the last name, so someone with a last name of Honda and a first name of Kenji would be addressed as Honda-**san**. Never use **san** to talk about yourself.

MAKING FRIENDS

Hello.	こんにちは *konnichi wa*
Pleased to meet you!	初めまして。 *hajimemashite*
Good morning.	おはようございます。 *ohayoo gozaimasu*

Good afternoon.	こんにちは。
	konnichi wa
Good evening.	こんばんは。
	konban wa
My name is…	…です。
	…desu
What's your name?	お名前は。
	onamae wa
I'd like to introduce you to…	…さんをご紹介します
	…san o goshookai shimasu
Nice to meet you.	よろしくお願いします。
	yoroshiku onegai shimasu
How are you?	お元気ですか。
	ogenki desu ka
Fine, thanks.	はい、おかげさまで。
	hai, okage sama de.
And you?	いかがですか。
	ikaga desu ka

Japanese has three levels of speech: plain, polite and honorific. Which level to use is determined by how well you know the other person, and also by age, social status and situation. Female speakers tend to employ polite speech, and young people often use plain speech. Japanese culture emphasizes respect, so honorific speech is appropriate when a younger person addresses an older person, or a person in an organization or company addresses a superior. Honorific speech is also used when trying to sell goods or services to others.

An appropriate greeting for the first meeting between adults is **Hajimemashite**, which literally means 'For the first time'. In subsequent meetings, this changes to **konnichi wa** (during the day) or **konban wa** (in the afternoon), which are still polite. **Yaa** (for men) and **Ara** (for women), both meaning Hi! are only appropriate among friends, in a casual setting.

In this book, you will find polite and honorific speech style.

YOU MAY SEE...

英語が少ししかできません。	I only speak a little English.
eego ga sukoshi shika dekimasen	
英語はできません。	I don't speak English.
eego wa dekimasen	

TRAVEL TALK

I'm here…	…で来ました。
	…dekimashita
on business	仕事
	shigoto
on vacation	観光 [休暇]
[holiday]	*kankoo [kyuuka]*
studying	研究
	kenkyuu
I'm staying for…	…間、滞在しています。
	…kan taizai shiteimasu
I've been here…	…前に、来ました。
	…mae ni kimashita
a day	日
	nichi/hi
a week	週
	shuu
a month	月
	tsuki
Where are you from?	どちらからですか。
	dochira kara desu ka
I'm from…	…から来ました。
	…kara kimashita

For Numbers, see page 20.

PERSONAL

Who are you with?	どなたとご一緒ですか。
	donata to goissho desu ka
I'm on my own.	一人です。
	hitori desu

I'm with my...	…と一緒です。
	…to issho desu
husband/wife	主人/家内
	shujin/kanai
boyfriend/	ボーイフレンド/ガールフレンド
girlfriend	*booifurendo/gaarufurendo*
friend(s)	友人
	yuujin
colleague(s)	同僚
	dooryoo
When's your birthday?	誕生日はいつですか。
	tanjoobi wa itsu desu ka
How old are you?	何歳ですか。
	nansai desu ka
I'm...	…歳です。
	…sai desu
Are you married?	結婚していますか。
	kekkon shite imasu ka
I'm...	私は
	… watashi wa…
single	ひとりです。
	hitori desu
in a relationship	付き合っています。
	tsukiatte imasu

engaged	…婚約中です。
	kon-yaku chuu desu
married	結婚しています。
	kekkon shite imasu
divorced	離婚しました。
	rikon shimashita
separated	別居中です。
	bekkyo chuu desu
I'm widowed.	妻/夫を亡くしました。
	tsuma f/otto m o nakushimashita
Do you have children/ grandchildren?	お子さん/お孫さんがいますか。
	okosan/omagosan ga imasu ka

WORK & SCHOOL

What do you do?	(お仕事は) 何をしていますか。
	(oshigoto wa)nani o shite imasu ka
What are you studying?	何を勉強していますか。
	nani o benkyoo shite imasu ka
I'm studying…	…を勉強しています。
	…o benkyoo shite imasu
I work full time/part time.	フルタイム/パートタイムです。
	furu/paato taimu desu
I'm between jobs.	求職中です。
	kyuushoku chuu desu
I work at home.	自宅で仕事をしています。
	jitaku de shigoto o shiteimasu
Who do you work for?	どちらにお勤めですか。
	dochira ni otsutome desu ka
I work for…	…に勤めています。
	…ni tsutomete imasu
Here's my business card.	名刺をどうぞ。
	meeshi o doozo

WEATHER

What's the weather forecast for tomorrow?	明日の予報は何ですか。 *ashita no yohoo wa nan desu ka*
What beautiful/ terrible weather!	なんてきれいな/いやな天気なんでしょう。 *nante kireina/iyana tenki nan deshoo*
It's cool/warm.	涼しい/暖かいです。 *suzushii/atatakai desu*
It's rainy/sunny.	雨/晴れです。 *ame/hare desu*
It's snowy/icy.	雪が降って/凍っています。 *yuki ga futte/kootte imasu*
Do I need a jacket/ an umbrella?	上着/傘がいりますか。 *uwagi/kasa ga irimasu ka*

Where is/are the...?	…はどこですか。
	...wa doko desu ka
exit	出口
	deguchi
taxis	タクシー
	takushii
Is there a...into town?	町に行く…はありますか。
	machi ni iku ...wa arimasu ka
bus	バス
	basu
train	電車
	densha
subway	地下鉄
	chikatetsu

For Asking Directions, see page 65.

TRAIN

How do I get to the train station?	駅には、どうやって行けますか。
	eki niwa doo yatte ikemasu ka
How far is it?	距離はどのくらいですか。
	kyori wa dono kurai desu ka
Where is/are the...?	…はどこですか。
	...wa doko desu ka
ticket office	きっぷうりば
	kippu uriba
information desk	受付
	uketsuke
luggage lockers	コインロッカー
	koin rokkaa
platforms	ホーム
	hoomu

LUGGAGE

Where is/are the...?　…はどこですか。
　　　　　　　　　　...wa doko desu ka

luggage carts [trolleys]	カート	*kaato*
luggage lockers	コインロッカー	*koin rokkaa*
baggage claim	荷物引渡場	*nimotsu hikiwatashijoo*

My luggage has been lost.　荷物がなくなりました。
　　　　　　　　　　nimotsu ga nakunarimashita

My luggage has been stolen.　荷物が盗まれました。
　　　　　　　　　　nimotsu ga nusumaremashita

My suitcase was damaged.　スーツケースが壊れています。
　　　　　　　　　　suutsukeesu ga kowarete imasu

A Travel Help Line is run by the Japan National Tourist Organization (JNTO). An English-speaking travel expert is available. Ask at your hotel or at a tourist information center for the phone number.

FINDING YOUR WAY

Where is/are the...?　…はどこですか。
　　　　　　　　　　...wa doko desu ka

currency exchange office	両替所	*ryoogaejo*
car rental [hire]	レンタカー	*rentakaa*

EXPLORING

GETTING AROUND

NEED TO KNOW

How do I get to town?	どうしたら町に行けますか。	
	dooshitara machi ni ikemasu ka	
How far is it?	距離はどのくらいですか。	
	kyori wa dono kurai desu ka	
Where can I buy tickets?	切符はどこで買えますか。	
	kippu wa doko de kaemasu ka	
Where's...?	...はどこですか。	
	...wa doko desu ka	
the airport	空港	
	kuukoo	
the train station	駅	
	eki	
the bus station	バスターミナル	
	basu taaminaru	
the subway [underground] station	地下鉄の駅	
	chikatetsu no eki	

Can you drive faster/ slower?	もっとはやく/ゆっくり 運転してくれませんか。
	motto hayaku/yukkuri unten shite kuremasenka

YOU MAY HEAR...

どの航空会社をご利用ですか。	What airline
dono kookuu gaisha o goriyoo desu ka	are you flying?
国内線ですか,国際線ですか。	Domestic or
kokunaisen desu ka kokusaisen desu ka	International?
どのターミナルですか。	What terminal?
dono taaminaru desu ka	

YOU MAY SEE...

到着	arrivals
toochaku	
出発	departures
shuppatsu	
荷物引渡場	baggage claim
nimotsu hikiwatashijoo	
国内線	domestic
kokunaisen	flights
国際線	international
kokusaisen	flights
チェックインデスク	check-in desk
chekku in desuku	
Eチケットチェックイン	e-ticket
e-chiketto chekku in	check-in
出発ゲート	departure
shuppatsu geeto	gates

A one-way [single]/ round-trip [return] ticket.	片道/往復
	katamichi/oofuku
How much?	いくらですか。
	ikura desuka
Are there any discounts?	割引料金はありますか。
	waribiki ryookin wa arimasu ka
Which...?	どちらの
	... dochira no...
gate	ゲート
	geeto
line	線
	sen
platform	ホーム
	hoomu
Where can I get a taxi?	タクシーはどこで乗れますか。
	takushii wa doko de noremasu ka
Please take me to this address.	この住所までお願いします。
	konojuusho made onegai shimasu
Where can I rent a car?	レンタカーはどこで借りられますか。
	rentakaa wa doko de kariraremasu ka
Can I have a map?	地図をお願いします。
	chizu o onegai shimasu

TICKETS

When's...to Kyoto?	京都行きの…は何時ですか。
	kyootoikino...wa nanji desu ka
the (first) bus	(始発)バス
	(shihatsu) basu
the (next) flight	(次の)便
	(tsugi no) bin

the last train	終電	
	shuuden	
Where can I buy tickets?	切符はどこで買えますか。	
	kippu wa doko de kaemasu ka	
One/Two ticket(s), please.	切符一枚/二枚お願いします。	
	kippu ichimai/nimai onegai shimasu	
For today/tomorrow.	今日/あしたの	
	kyoo/ashita no	
A…ticket	…チケット	
	…chiketto	
one-way [single]	片道	
	katamichi	
round-trip [return]	往復	
	oofuku	
first class	ファーストクラス	
	faasuto kurasu	
business class	ビジネス・クラス	
	bijinesu kurasu	
economy class	エコノミー	
	ekonomii	
How much?	いくらですか。	
	ikura desuka	
Is there a discount for…?	…割引はありますか。	
	…waribiki wa arimasu ka	
children	子供の	
	kodomo no	
students	学生	
	gakusee	
senior citizens	高齢者	
	kooreesha	
tourists	観光客向けの	
	kankookyaku mukeno	
The express bus/ express train, please.	高速バス/特急電車をお願いします。	
	koosoku basu/tokkyuu densha o onegai shimasu	

The local bus/ train, please.	路線バス/普通電車をお願いします。	
	rosen basu/futsuu densha o onegai shimasu	
I have an e-ticket.	Eチケットがあります。	
	iichiketto ga arimasu	
Can I buy a ticket on the bus/train?	バス/電車 の中で切符が買えますか。	
	basu/densha no nakade kippu ga kaemasu ka	
I'd like to…my reservation.	予約を…したいんですが。	
	yoyaku o …shitian desu ga	
cancel	キャンセル	
	kyanseru	
change	変更	
	henkoo	
confirm	確認	
	kakunin	

For Days, see page 26.

AIRPORT TRANSFER

How much is a taxi to the airport?	空港までタクシーはいくらですか。	
	kuukoo made takushii wa ikura desu ka	
To…Airport, please.	…空港までお願いします。	
	…kuukoo made onegai shimasu	
My airline is…	航空会社は…です。	
	kookuu gaisha wa…desu	
My flight leaves at…	飛行機の便は…に出ます。	
	hikooki no bin wa… ni demasu	
I'm in a rush.	急いでいます 。	
	isoide imasu	
Can you take an alternate route?	他の道を行ってください。	
	hoka no michi o itte kudasai	

CHECKING IN

Where is the check-in desk for flight...?	...便のチェックインデスクはどこですか。
	...bin no chekkuin desuku wa doko desu ka
My name is...	...です。
	...desu
I'm going to...	...へ行きます。
	...e ikimasu
How much luggage is allowed?	荷物はどれくらい持ち込めますか。
	nimotsu wa dore kurai mochikomemasu ka
Which gate does flight... leave from?	...便のゲートは何番ですか。
	... bin no geeto wa nanban desu ka
I'd like a window/an aisle seat.	窓側/通路側の席をお願いします。
	madogawa/tsuurogawa no seki o onegaishimasu
When do we leave/ arrive?	何時に出ますか/着きますか。
	nanji ni demasu ka/tsukimasu ka
Is flight...delayed?	...便は遅れていますか。
	...bin wa okurete imasu ka
How late will it be?	どのくらい遅れますか。
	dono kurai okuremasu ka

YOU MAY HEAR...

次の方
tsugi no kata
Next!

チケット/パスポートをお見せください。
chiketto/pasupooto o omise kudasai
Your ticket/ passport, please.

お荷物はいくつありますか。
onimotsu wa ikutsu arimasu ka
How many pieces of luggage do you have?

重量超過です。
juuryoo chooka desu
You have excess baggage.

それは手荷物には重すぎます/ 大きすぎます。
sore wa tenimostu ni wa omosugimasu/ ookisugimasu
That's too heavy/large for a carry-on [to carry on board].

お荷物は、ご自分で詰められましたか。
onimotsu wa gojibun de tsumeraremashita ka
Did you pack these bags yourself?

誰かに何か運ぶように頼まれましたか。
dareka ni nanika hakobuyooni tanomaremashita ka
Did anyone give you anything to carry?

ポケットのものを出してください。
poketto no mono o dashite kudasai
Empty your pockets.

靴を脱いでください。
kutsu o nuide kudasai
Take off your shoes.

...便のお客様はご搭乗いただきます。
...bin no okyakusama wa gotoojoo itadakimasu
Now boarding flight...

Can I have a schedule [timetable]?	時刻表をください。
	jikokuhyoo o kudasai
How long is the trip?	どのくらいかかりますか。
	dono kurai kakarimasu ka
Is it a direct train?	この電車は直行便ですか。
	kono densha wa chokkoobin desu ka
Do I have to change trains?	乗り換えはありますか。
	norikae wa arimasu ka
Is the train on time?	電車は時間通りですか。
	densya wa jikandoori desu ka

For Time, see page 25.

YOU MAY SEE…

ホーム	platforms
案内係	information
予約窓口	reservations
到着	arrivals
出発	departures

Japan's rail network covers the whole country. There are many different rail operators, and the service is clean, safe, and punctual. First-class cars are called **guriin sha** (green cars) and are marked with a green four-leaf sign. To travel first class you need a special ticket in addition to the normal ticket. Second-class cars have reserved seats and unreserved seats. Reserved seats are a little more expensive. The types of train are:

新幹線 **shinkansen**, the bullet train. This is the fastest rail service. There are lines in Honshu (main island), Kyushu (south island), and Hokkaido (north island). There are three types: **Nozomi** (the fastest train), **Hikari** and **Kodama**.

特急 **tokkyuu**, limited express. This service is for long-distance travel.

急行 **kyuuko**, the ordinary medium-distance express.

快速 **kaisoku**, rapid train. This commuter service has no surcharge above the basic fare.

普通 **futsuu**, local train. This commuter service has no surcharge above the basic fare.

Tourists can buy special passes for unlimited travel on the rail system, as well as on buses and ferries, throughout Japan. These passes must be bought outside Japan, from offices of Japan Air Lines, travel agents, or Japan Travel Bureau offices. There are a number of other special discounts for travel along certain lines within designated areas over a set period, for example **Shuuyuuken** (周遊券), **Free kippu** (フリーきっぷ), and **Parent-Child Super Pass** (親子スーパーパス). Enquire about these tickets at station travel shops.

Most tickets are bought from vending machines. Find your destination on the diagram above the machines, insert money (change is given), and press the button for the appropriate amount. The station names on the diagram are usually in Japanese only, so it is important to know the characters of the station you are going to.

DEPARTURES

Which track [platform] for the train to…?	…行きの列車は何番ホームですか。 *…iki no ressha wa nan-ban hoomu desu ka*
Is this the track [platform] to…?	…行きのホームはここですか。 *… iki no hoomu wa koko desu ka*
Where is track [platform]…?	…行きのホームはどこですか。 *… iki no hoomu wa doko desu ka*
Where do I change for…?	…へ行くには、どこで乗り換えますか。 *…e ikuniwa doko de norikaemasu ka*

YOU MAY HEAR…

ご乗車の方はお急ぎください。 *gojoosha no kata wa oisogi kudasai*	All aboard!
乗車券を拝見します。 *jooshaken o haiken shimasu*	Tickets, please.
…で乗り換えてください。 *…de norikaete kudasai*	You have to change at…
次の停車駅は *…tsugi no teishaeki wa …*	Next stop…

ON BOARD

Can I sit here?	ここに座ってもいいですか。 *koko ni suwattemo iidesuka*
Can I open the window?	窓を開けてもいいですか。 *mado o aketemo iidesu ka*
Is this seat taken?	この席は空いていますか。 *kono seki wa aite imasu ka*

That's my seat.	そこは私の席です。
	soko wa watashi no seki desu
Here's my reservation.	こちらが予約票です。
	kochira ga yoyakuhyoo desu

BUS

Where's the bus station?	バスのターミナルはどこですか。
	basu no taaminaru wa doko desu ka
How far is it?	距離はどのくらいですか。
	kyori wa dono kurai desu ka
How do I get to…?	どうしたら…に行けますか。
	dooshitara…ni ikemasu ka
Does the bus stop at…?	…に止まりますか。
	…ni tomarimasu ka
Could you tell me when to get off?	下りる場所が来たら、教えてください。
	oriru basho ga kitara oshiete kudasai
Do I have to change buses?	乗り換えはありますか。
	norikae wa arimasu ka
Stop here, please!	ここで止めてください。
	kokode tomete kudasai

For Tickets, see page 47.

There are extensive city and rural bus services
in Japan. Some towns, such as Hakone, Nagasaki and
Kumamoto, have streetcars [trams]. When you board a bus
take a numbered ticket and pay at the end. You can save
money by buying **kaisuuken**, multiple-ride tickets.

YOU MAY SEE...

| バス停留所/バス停 | bus stop |
| 入口/出口 | enter/exit |

SUBWAY

Where's the nearest Subway station?
最寄りの地下鉄の駅はどこですか。
moyori no chikatetsu no eki wa doko desu ka

Could I have a map of the subway, please?
地下鉄の路線図をください。
chikatetsu no rosenzu o kudasai

Which line for...?
…は、何線ですか。
...wa nanisen desu ka

Which direction?
どこ行きですか。
doko iki desu ka

Do I have to transfer [change]?
乗り換えが必要ですか。
norikae ga hitsuyoo desu ka

Is this the subway [train] to...?
この電車は
…へ行きますか。
kono densha wa...e ikimasu ka

Tokyo, Osaka, Nagoya and other big cities have very efficient subway systems. A map showing the various lines and stations is displayed outside **chikatetsu**, subway stations. Trains are frequent and run until around midnight. Station platform signs are in Japanese and English. Avoid rush hours (7:00 - 9:00 a.m. and 5:00 - 7:00 p.m.), when trains can be extremely crowded.

How many stops to...?	…までの停車駅はいくつですか。
	… made no teesya eki wa ikutsu desu ka
Where are we?	ここは、どこですか。
	koko wa doko desu ka

BOAT & FERRY

When is the car ferry to Okinawa?	沖縄行きのカーフェリーは、何時ですか。
	okinawa iki no kaa ferii wa nanji desu ka
What time is the next sailing?	次の出航は何時ですか。
	tsugi no syukkoo wa nanji desu ka
Can I book a seat/ cabin?	座席/船室を予約したいんですが。
	zaseki/senshitsu o yoyaku shitain desu ga
How long is the crossing?	到着までどのくらいかかりますか。
	toochaku made dono kurai kakarimasu ka

For Tickets, see page 47.

Ferry services run from Honshu (the main island) to the other islands. Details about ports and sailings may be obtained from the Tourist Information Center (TIC). To sample the charms of the Inland Sea, travel by ferry or hydrofoil is recommended.

Various cruises are available in the Tokyo Bay area, many departing from Hinode Pier (日の出桟橋 **hinode sanbashi**). In Kobe, travelers may enjoy 50-minute port cruises departing from Naka Pier. In Yokohama, you can find 50-minute tours of the harbor leaving from near the retired cruise liner, Hikawa Maru.

TAXI

Where can I get a taxi?	タクシーはどこで乗れますか。
	takushii wa doko de noremasu ka
I'd like a taxi now/ for tomorrow.	今/ 明日 タクシーをお願いします。
	ima/ashita takushii o onegai shimasu
Do you have the number for a taxi?	タクシー会社の電話番号をご存知ですか。
	takushii gaisha no denwa bangoo o gozonji desu ka
Can you send a taxi?	タクシーを呼んでもらえますか。
	takushii o yonde morae masu ka
Pick me up at (place/time).	(place)に/(time)に来てください。
	...ni kite kudasai
I'm going to...	...へ行きます。
	...e ikimasu
this address	この住所
	kono juusho
the airport	空港
	kuukoo
the train [railway] station	駅
	eki
I'm late.	急いでいるんです。
	isoide irun desu
Can you drive faster/ slower?	急いで/ゆっくり運転してください。
	isoide/yukkuri unten shite kudasai

YOU MAY HEAR...

どちらまで。	Where to?
dochira made	
ご住所は。	What's the address?
gojuusho wa	

Stop/Wait here.	ここで止めて/待っていてください。
	kokode tomete/matteite kudasai
How much?	いくらですか。
	ikura desuka
You said it would cost...yen.	…円ですね。
	...en desu ne
Keep the change.	お釣りは結構です。
	otsuri wa kekkoo desu
A receipt, please.	レシートをお願いします。
	reshiito o onegai shimasu

Taxis are usually yellow or green. If the light in the bottom right-hand corner of the windshield is red, the taxi is free; if it's green, it's occupied. The rear doors are remote controlled — be careful not to get knocked over by them! Few taxi drivers speak English, so have your destination written down on paper. Taxi drivers do not expect to be tipped.

BICYCLE & MOTORBIKE

I'd like to rent...	…を借りたいんですが。
	...o karitain desu ga
a 3-/10-speed bicycle	3速/10速の自転車
	sansoku/jussoku no jitensha
a moped	スクーター
	sukuutaa
a motorcycle	オートバイ
	ootobai
How much per day/week?	一日/一週間、いくらですか。いくらですか。
	ichinichi/isshuukan ikura desu ka

Can I have a helmet/ lock?	ヘルメット/ロックをお願いします。
	herumetto/rokku o onegai shimasu
I have a puncture/ flat tyre.	タイヤがパンクしています。
	taiya ga panku shite imasu

CAR HIRE

Where can I rent a car?	レンタカーはどこで借りられますか。
	rentakaa wa doko de kariraremasu ka
I'd like to rent...	…を借りたいんですが。
	...o karitain desu ga
a 2-/4-door car	2/4ドア車
	tsuu/foo doa sha
an automatic	オートマチック
	ootomachikku
a car with air conditioning	エアコン付の車
	eakon tsuki no kuruma
a car seat	チャイルドシート
	chairudo shiito
How much...?	いくら
	ikura
per day/week	一日/一週間
	ichinichi/isshuukan
per kilometer	一キロ
	ichi kiro
for unlimited mileage	距離は無制限で
	kyori wa museigen de
with insurance	保険付きで
	hoken tsuki de
Are there any special weekend rates?	週末料金はありますか。
	shuumatsu ryookin wa arimasu ka
(Where's) the parking meter?	パーキングメーター (はどこです か。)
	paakingu meetaa (wa doko desu ka)
(Where's...) the parking garage?	駐車場 (はどこですか。)
	chuushajoo (wa doko desu ka)

YOU MAY HEAR...

国際免許証をお持ちですか。
kokusai menkyoshoo o omochi desu ka

パスポートをお見せください。
pasupooto o omise kudasai
保険をお掛けになりますか。
hoken o okakeni narimasu ka
…の前金をいただきます。
…no maekin o itadakimasu
ここにサインをお願いします。
koko ni sain o onegai shimasu

Do you have an
international
driver's
license?
Your passport,
please.
Do you want
insurance?
There is a
deposit of…
Please sign
here.

FUEL STATION

Where's the fuel station?	ガソリンスタンドはどこですか。
	gasorin sutando wa doko desu ka
Fill it up, please.	満タンにしてください。
	mantan ni shite kudasai
…liters, please.	…リットルお願いします。
	…rittoru onegai shimasu
I'll pay in cash/by credit card.	現金/(クレジット)カードで払います。
	genkin/(kurejitto) kaado de haraimasu

YOU MAY SEE…

レギュラー	regular
スーパー	premium [super]
ディーゼル	diesel

ASKING DIRECTIONS

Is this the right road to…?	…に行くのは、この道でいいんですか。
	…ni ikuno wa kono michi de iin desu ka
How far is it to…?	…まで、どのくらいありますか。
	…made donokurai arimasu ka
Where's…?	…はどこですか。
	…wa doko desu ka
…Street	…通り
	…doori
this address	この住所
	kono juusho
the highway [motorway]	高速道路
	koosoku dooro

Can you show me on the map?
I'm lost.

この地図で教えてください。
kono chizu de oshiete kudasai
道に迷いました。
michi ni mayoimashita

YOU MAY HEAR...

まっすぐ *massugu*	straight ahead
左 *hidari*	left
右 *migi*	right
角/道を曲がったところ *kado/michi o magatta tokoro*	on/around the corner
向かい *mukai*	across
後ろ *ushiro*	behind
のとなり *no tonari*	next to
北/南 *kita/minami*	north/south
東/西 *higashi/nishi*	east/west
信号 *shingoo*	traffic light
交差点 *koosaten*	intersection

YOU MAY SEE...

 stop

 slow down

 minimum speed

 time-limited parking

 no standing

 no parking

 dangerous curve

 one way

 no entry

PARKING

Can I park here?	ここに駐車してもいいですか。 *koko ni chuusha shitemo ii desu ka*
Where is the nearest parking garage?	この近くに駐車場はありますか。 *kono chikaku ni chuushajoo wa arimasu ka*
How much...?	…いくらですか。 *...ikura desuka*
per hour	一時間 *ichijikan*
per day	一日 *ichinichi*
overnight	一晩 *hitoban*
(Where's) the parking meter?	パーキングメーター（はどこですか。） *paakingu meetaa (wa doko desu ka)*

Street parking is limited. It is common to have your
car towed away or booted if you park in illegal spaces. It is
an expensive and time-consuming process to get it back.
Some hotels have parking facilities, otherwise the best
solution is to use designated parking garages.

BREAKDOWN & REPAIR

My car broke down/ won't start.	車が壊れました。/スタートしません。 *kuruma ga kowaremashita/sutaato shimasen*
Can you fix it?	直してもらえませんか。 *naoshite moraemasen ka*
When will it be ready?	いつ直りますか。 *itsu naorimasu ka*
How much?	いくらですか。 *ikura desuka*
I have a puncture/ flat tyre.	タイヤがパンクしています。 *taiya ga panku shite imasu*

ACCIDENTS

There has been an accident.	事故がありました。 *jiko ga arimashita*
Call an ambulance/ the police.	警察/救急車を呼んでください。 *keesatsu/kyuukyuusha o yonde kudasai*

PLACES TO STAY

NEED TO KNOW

Can you recommend a hotel in...?	…で良いホテルを教えてください。 *…de ii hoteru o oshiete kudasai*
I have a reservation.	予約してあります。 *yoyaku shite arimasu*
My name is...	…です。 *…desu*
Do you have a room...?	…部屋はありますか。 *…heya wa arimasu ka*
with a bathroom	バス付きの *basu tsuki no*
with AC	エアコン付きの *eakon tsuki no*
Do you have a room for one/two?	一人/二人部屋はありますか。 *hitori/futari beya wa arimasuka*
For tonight	今晩 *konban*

For two nights	二晩
	futaban
For one week	一週間
	isshuukan
How much?	いくらですか。
	ikura desuka
Is there anything cheaper?	もっと安い部屋はありますか。
	motto yasui heya wa arimasu ka
When's check-out?	チェックアウトは何時ですか。
	chekkuautowa nanji desu ka
Can I leave this in the safe?	これを金庫に預けたいんですが。
	kore o kinko ni azuketain desu ga
Can I leave my bags?	荷物を預けたいんですが。
	nimotsu o azuketain desu ga
Can I have the bill/a receipt?	レシート/会計をお願いします。
	kaikee/reshiito o onegai shimasu
I'll pay in cash/by credit card.	現金/(クレジット)カードで払います。
	genkin/(kurejitto) kaado de haraimasu

SOMEWHERE TO STAY

Can you recommend a hotel?	いホテルを教えてください。
	iihoteruooshiete kudasai
Can you recommend a capsule hotel?	どこか良いカプセルホテルはありますか。
	dokoka yoi kapuseru hoteru wa arimasu ka
Can you recommend a hostel?	どこか良い ホステル はありますか 。
	dokoka yoi hosuteru wa arimasu ka
Can you recommend a campsite?	どこか良い キャンプ場 はありますか 。
	dokoka yoi kyanpujoo wa arimasu ka
Can you recommend a bed and breakfast?	どこか良い 民宿 はありますか 。
	dokoka yoi minsyuku wa arimasu ka

Can you recommend an inn?	どこか良い旅館はありますか 。
	dokoka yoi ryokan wa arimasu ka
What is it near?	どこの近くですか。
	doko no chikaku desu ka
How do I get there?	どうやって行くんですか。
	dooyatte ikun desu ka

There are many different places to stay in Japan.
ホテル **hoteru** are Western-style hotels. These are
comparable to western hotels.
ビジネスホテル **bijinesu hoteru**, or business hotels, have
small rooms, often with no room service. They are clean
and comfortable and usually located near train stations.
旅館 **ryokan** are Japanese-style inns. For a taste of the
Japanese way of life, a stay at a **ryokan** is recommended.
Many are situated in beautiful settings with access to hot
springs. Room prices include breakfast, dinner, and service
charge. The majority offer only traditional style bathrooms,
meals and sleeping arrangements.
Another good way of sampling authentic Japanese lodgings
is a 民宿 **minshuku**, or guest house. **Minshuku** are often
family run and have an informal, friendly atmosphere. The
overnight charge includes dinner and breakfast.
For those with a particular interest in Buddhism, 宿防
shukuboo, temple accommodation, will allow you to join in
the monks' daily life.

AT THE HOTEL

I have a reservation.	予約してあります。
	yoyaku shite arimasu

My name is...	…です。
	…desu
Do you have a room...?	…部屋はありますか。
	…heya wa arimasu ka
with a bathroom [toilet]/shower	バス/シャワー付きの
	basu/shawaa tukino
with AC	エアコンつきの
	eakon tsuki no
that's smoking/ non-smoking	喫煙/禁煙の
	kitsuen/kinen no
for tonight	今晩
	konban
for two nights	二晩
	futaban
for one week	一週間
	isshuukan
Does the hotel have...?	ホテルに…はありますか。
	hoteru ni… wa arimasu ka
a computer	コンピュータ
	konpyuuta
an elevator [lift]	エレベーター
	erebeetaa
(wireless) internet service	(ワイアレス)インターネットサービス
	(waiaresu) intaanetto saabisu
room service	ルームサービス
	ruumu saabisu
a gym	フィットネスセンター
	fittonesu sentaa
a pool	プール
	puuru
I need...	…が要るんですが。
	…ga irun desu ga
an extra bed	もう一つベッド
	moo hitotsu beddo

a cot	折り畳みベッド
	oritatami beddo
a crib [child's cot]	ベビーベッド
	bebii beddo

YOU MAY HEAR...

パスポート/カードをお願いします。
pasupooto/kaado o onegai shimasu

この用紙にご記入ください。
kono yooshi ni gokinyuu kudasai
ここにサインをお願いします。
koko ni sain o onegai shimasu

Your passport/
credit card
please.
Please fill out
this form.
Sign here.

PRICE

How much per night/ week?	一泊/一週間いくらですか。
	ippaku/isshuukan ikura desu ka
Does the price include breakfast/ sales tax [VAT]?	この料金は朝食/消費税込みですか。
	kono ryookin wa chooshoku/shoohi zee komi desu ka

PREFERENCES

Can I see the room?	部屋を見せてもらえますか。
	heya o misete morae masu ka
I'd like a...room.	…部屋にしてもらえますか。
	...heya ni shite morae masu ka
better	もっと良い
	motto yoi

bigger	もっと大きい
	motto ookii
cheaper	もっと安い
	motto yasui
quieter	もっと静かな
	motto shizuka na
I'll take it.	それにします。
	sore ni shimasu
No, I won't take it.	いいえ、結構です。
	Iie kekkou desu

QUESTIONS

Where's the...?	…はどこですか。
	...wa doko desu ka
bar	バー
	baa
bathroom [toilet]	トイレ
	toire
elevator [lift]	エレベーター
	erebeetaa
Can I have...?	…をお願いします。
	...o onegai shimasu
a blanket	毛布
	moofu
an iron	アイロン
	airon
the room key	ルームキー
	ruumu kii
key card	キーカード
	kii kaado
a pillow	枕
	makura

soap	石鹸 *sekken*
toilet paper	トイレットペーパー *toiretto peepaa*
a towel	タオル *taoru*
Do you have an adapter for this?	アダプタはありますか。 *adaputa wa arimasu ka*
How do I turn on the lights?	電気はどうやって付けますか。 *denki wa dooyatte tsukemasu ka*
Could you wake me at…?	…時に起こしてください。 *…ji ni okoshite kudasai*
Can I leave this in the safe?	これを金庫に保管できますか。 *kore o kinko ni hokan dekimasu ka*
Could I have my things from the safe?	私のものを金庫から出してください。 *watashi no mono o kinko kara dashite kudasai*
Is/are there any mail/messages for me?	手紙/メッセージがありますか。 *tegami/messeeji ga arimasu ka*
Do you have a laundry service?	ランドリーサービスはありますか。 *randorii saabisu wa arimasu ka*

There are two types of toilet you may find in Japan. Traditional Japanese squat toilets have nothing to sit down on, and the user squats down to use the facility. These toilets flush just like western style. You will also find some toilets like you see in the West. Western style toilets may range from very basic to a high-tech model which will have a heated seat, water jets to wash and warm air to dry, and an automatic mechanism to flush and close the lid.

YOU MAY SEE...   👁

押す/引く	push/pull
トイレ	restroom [toilet]
シャワー	shower
エレベーター	elevator [lift]
階段	stairs
洗濯室	laundry
起こさないでください	do not disturb
防火扉	fire door
非常口	(emergency) exit
モーニングコール	wake-up call

PROBLEMS

There's a problem.	ちょっと困っているんですが。
	chotto komatte irun desu ga
I've lost my key/key card.	鍵/カードキーをなくしました。
	kagi/kaado kii o nakushimashita
I've locked myself out of my room.	鍵を部屋に置いたまま出てきてしまいました。
	kagi o heya ni oitamama detekite shimaimashita
There's no hot water/toilet paper.	お湯/トイレットペーパーがないんですが。
	oyu/toiretto peepaa ga nain desuga
The room is dirty.	部屋が汚いんですが。
	heya ga kitanain desu ga
There are bugs in our room.	部屋に虫がいるんですが。
	heya ni mushi ga irun desuga
The...has broken down.	…が壊れたんですが。
	...ga kowaretan desuga

Can you fix...?	…を直してもらえますか。
	...o naoshite moraemasu ka
the AC	エアコン
	eakon
the fan	扇風機
	senpuuki
the heat [heating]	暖房
	danboo
the light	電気
	denki
the TV	テレビ
	terebi
the toilet	トイレ
	toire
I'd like to move to another room.	部屋を替えてください。
	heya o kaete kudasai

(i)

Japan uses the 100 volt electricity system. You may need a converter and/or adapter for your appliances.

CHECKING OUT

When's check-out?	チェックアウトは何時ですか。
	chekkuauto wa nanji desu ka
Could I leave my bags here until…?	…まで荷物を置いておいてもいいですか。
	…made nimotsu o oite oitemo ii desu ka
Can I have an itemized bill/a receipt?	明細書/レシートをお願いします。
	meesaisho/reshiito o onegai shimasu
I think there's a mistake in this bill.	この会計は違っているようですが。
	kono kaikee wa chigatte iru yoo desu ga
I'll pay in cash/by credit card.	現金/(クレジット)カードで払います。
	genkin/(kurejitto) kaado de haraimasu

> (i)
>
> Tipping isn't customary and is officially discouraged. Porters at airports and train stations charge a set fee. Hotels, **ryokan** (Japanese inns) and restaurants add a 10-15% service charge to the bill.

RENTING

I've reserved an apartment/a room.	アパート/部屋を借りました。
	apaato/heya o karimashita
My name is…	…です。
	…desu
Can I have the key/key card?	鍵/カードキーをお願いします。
	kagi/kaado kii o onegai shimasu
Are there…?	…はありますか
	…wa arimasu ka
dishes and utensils	食器
	shokki

pillows	枕	
	makura	
Are there...?	…はありますか。	
	...wa arimasu ka	
sheets	シーツ	
	shiitsu	
towels	タオル	
	taoru	
When/Where do I put out the trash [rubbish]?	ゴミはどこへ/いつ出すんですか。	
	gomi wa doko e/itsu dasun desu ka	
...is broken.	…が壊れているんですが。	
	...ga kowarete irun desuga	
How does...work?	…はどうやって使えばいいんですか。	
	...wa dooyatte tsukaeba ii n desu ka	
the air-conditioner	エアコン	
	eakon	
the dishwasher	食洗機	
	shokusen ki	
the freezer	冷凍庫	
	reetooko	
the heater	ヒーター	
	hiitaa	
the microwave	電子レンジ	
	denshi renji	
the refrigerator	冷蔵庫	
	reezooko	
the stove	コンロ	
	konro	
the washing machine	洗濯機	
	sentakuki	

DOMESTIC ITEMS

I need...	…が要るんですが。
	…ga irun desu ga
an adapter	アダプタ
	adaputa
aluminum	アルミホイル
[kitchen] foil	*arumi hoiru*
a bottle opener	栓抜き
	sen nuki
a broom	箒
	hooki
a can opener	缶切り
	kankiri
cleaning supplies	クリーニング用品
	kuriiningu yoohin
a corkscrew	コルクスクリュー
	koruku sukuryuu
detergent	洗剤
	senzai
dishwashing liquid	中性洗剤
	tyuusee senzai
garbage [rubbish]	ごみ袋
bags	*gomi bukuro*

a light bulb	電球
	denkyuu
matches	マッチ
	matchi
a mop	モップ
	moppu
napkins	ナプキン
	napukin
paper towels	ペーパータオル
	peepaa taoru
plastic wrap [cling film]	ラップ
	rappu
a plunger	トイレの吸引具
	toire no kyuuingu
scissors	はさみ
	hasami
a vacuum cleaner	掃除機
	soojiki

For In the Kitchen, see page 185.

AT THE HOSTEL

Do you have any places left for tonight?	今晩、空いている部屋はありますか。
	konban aiteiru heya wa arimasuka
Can I have…?	…をお願いします。
	…o onegai shimasu
a single/ double room	一人/二人部屋
	hitori/futari beya
a blanket	毛布
	moofu
a pillow	枕
	makura

sheets	シーツ
	shiitsu
a towel	タオル
	taoru
Do you have lockers?	ロッカーはありますか。
	rokkaa wa arimasu ka
What time do you lock up?	正面玄関は、何時に閉まりますか。
	shoomen genkan wa nanji ni shimarimasu ka
Do I need a membership card?	メンバーシップカードは必要です か。
	menbaa shippu kaado wa hitsuyoo desu ka
Here's my international student card.	こちらが国際学生証です。
	kochira ga kokusai gakusei shoo desu

> There are over 500 youth hostels, or ユースホステル **yuusu hosuteru**, located in every part of Japan. They offer the most inexpensive accommodations available. You will often need to share rooms or bathrooms.

GOING CAMPING

Can I camp here?	ここでキャンプできますか。
	koko de kyanpu dekimasu ka
Is there a campsite near here?	この近くに、キャンプ場はありますか。
	kono chikaku ni kyanpujoo wa arimasu ka
What is the charge per day/week?	一日/一週間の料金はいくらですか。
	ichi-nichi/isshuukan no ryookin wa ikura desu ka

Are there...?	…はありますか 。
	...wa arimasu ka
cooking facilities	炊事場
	suijiba
electrical outlets	電源
	dengen
laundry facilities	洗濯場
	sentakuba
showers	シャワー
	shawaa
tents for hire	貸しテント
	kashi tento
Where can I empty the chemical toilet?	ケミカルトイレの汚物を処理したいんです が。
	kemikaru toire no obutsu o shori shitain desu ga

For Domestic Items, see page 80.

YOU MAY SEE...

飲料水	drinking water
キャンプ禁止	no camping
焚火/バーベキュー禁止	no fires/ barbecues

COMMUNICATIONS

NEED TO KNOW

Where's an internet café?	インターネットカフェはどこですか。 *intaanetto kafe wa doko desu ka*
Can I access the internet/check e-mail?	インターネット/E メールを使いたいんです が。 *intaanetto/iimeeru o tsukaitain desu ga*
How much per (half) hour?	一(半)時間いくらですか。 *ichi(han)jikan ikura desu ka*
How do I connect / log on?	接続/ログオンしたいんですが。 *setsuzoku/roguon shitain desu ga*
I'd like a phone card, please.	テレホンカードをください。 *terehon kaado o kudasai*
Can I have your phone number?	電話番号を教えてください。 *denwa bangoo o oshiete kudasai*
Here's my number/ e-mail address.	これが私の電話番号/E メールアドレ スです。 *kore ga watashi no denwabangoo/ iimeeru adoresu desu*
Call me.	電話してください。 *denwa shite kudasai*
E-mail me.	メールをください。 *meeru o kudasai*
Hello. This is…	もしもし。…ですが。 *moshi moshi…desu ga*
I'd like to speak to…	…さん、お願いします。 *…san onegai shimasu*
Could you repeat that, please?	もう一度、言ってください。 *moo ichido itte kudasai*

公衆電話

I'll call back later.	あとで電話します。
	ato de denwa shimasu
Bye.	ごめんください。
	gomen kudasai
Where's the post office?	郵便局はどこですか。
	yuubinkyoku wa doko desu ka
I'd like to send this to…	これを…に送りたいんですが。
	kore o…ni okuri tain desu ga

ONLINE

Where's an internet cafe?	インターネットカフェはどこですか。
	intaanetto kafe wa doko desu ka
Does it have wireless internet?	ワイアレスインターネットがありますか。
	waiaresu intaanetto ga arimasu ka
How do I turn the computer on/off?	コンピュータを点け/消したいんですが。
	konpyuuta o tsuke/keshi tain desu ga
What is the WiFi password?	無線LANのパスワードは何ですか。
	musen LAN no pasuwaado wa nandesuka
Is the WiFi free?	無線LAN は無料ですか 。
	musen LAN wa muryoo desuka

Can I access Skype?	スカイプにアクセスできますか
	sukaipu ni akusesu deki masu ka
Do you have bluetooth?	Bluetooth はありますか
	bluu twuusu wa ari masu ka
Can I...?	…いいですか。
	...iidesuka
plug in/charge my laptop/iPhone/iPad?	ラップトップ /iPhone/iPad の電源をつないでも/を充電しても
	rapputoppu/ai fon/ai paddo no dengen o tsunaidemo/o juuden shitemo
Can I...?	…ができますか。
	...ga dekimasu ka
access the internet	インターネットアクセス
	intaanetto akusesu
check e-mail	E メールのチェック
	iimeeru no chekku
print	印刷
	insatsu
How much per (half) hour?	一(半)時間いくらですか。
	ichi(han)jikan ikura desu ka
How do I...?	…はどうしますか。
	...wa doo shimasu ka
connect	接続する
	setsuzoku suru
disconnect	接続を切るの
	setsuzoku o kiru no
log on/off	ログオン/ログオフするの
	roguon/roguofu suru no
type this symbol	この記号をタイプするの
	kono kigoo o taipu suru no
What's your e-mail?	E メールのアドレスは何ですか。
	iimeeru no adoresuwa nan desu ka

My e-mail is...	私のEメールアドレスは…
	watashi no iimeeru adoresu wa...
Do you have a scanner?	スキャナーはありますか。
	sukyanaa wa arimasu ka

SOCIAL MEDIA

Are you on Facebook/Twitter?	Facebook/Twitter に参加していますか。
	feisu bukku/tsuittaa ni sanka shite imasu ka
What's your user name?	ユーザーネームは何ですか。
	yuuzaa neemu wa nan desu ka
I'll add you as a friend.	友達に追加します。
	tomodachi ni tsuika shimasu
I'll follow you on Twitter.	Twitter でフォローします。
	tsuittaa de foroo shimasu
Are you following...?	…をフォローしていますか。
	...o foroo shite imasu ka
I'll put the pictures on Facebook/ Twitter.	Facebook/Twitter に写真を載せます。
	feisu bukku / tsuittaa ni shashin o nose masu
I'll tag you in the pictures.	あなたの写真にタグをつけます。
	anatano shashin ni tagu o tsuke masu

YOU MAY SEE...

閉じる	close
削除する	delete
Eメール	e-mail
ログアウト	exit
ヘルプ	help
インスタント・メッセージ	instant messenger
インターネット	internet
ログイン	login
新着メール	new (message)
オン/オフ	on/off
開ける	open
印刷する	print
保存	save
送信	send
ユーザー名/パスワード	username/ password
無線インターネット/ ワイヤレスインター ネット	wireless internet

PHONE

A phonecard/ prepaid phone, please.	テレホンカード/プリペイド携帯をお願いします。 *terehonkaado/puripeidokeitai o onegai shimasu*
How much?	いくらですか。 *ikura desuka*
What's the area/ country code for...?	…の市外局番/国番号は何番ですか。 *...no shigaikyokuban/kunibangoo wa nanban desu ka*

What's the number for Information?	番号案内は何番ですか。
	bangoo an-nai wa nanban desu ka
I'd like the number for...	…の番号を教えてください。
	...no bangooo oshiete kudasai
Where's the pay phone?	公衆電話はどこですか。
	koosyuu denwa wa doko desu ka
My phone doesn't work here.	私の電話が使えません。
	watashi no denwa ga tsukaemasen
What network are you on?	どの電話会社をご使用ですか。
	dono denwa gaisha o goshiyoo desu ka
Is it 3G?	3Gですか。
	3G desu ka
I have run out of credit/minutes.	クレジット/分数を使い果たしてしまいました。
	kurejitto/funsuu o tsukai hatashite shimai mashita
Can I buy some credit?	クレジットを買いたいのですが。
	kurejitto o kaitai no desu ga
A prepaid phone, please.	プリペイドフォンをお願いします。
	puripeido fon o onegai shimasu
Do you have a phone charger?	携帯用の充電器はありますか。
	keitaiyoo no juudenki wa arimasu ka
Can I have your number?	電話番号を教えてください。
	denwa bangoo o oshiete kudasai
Here's my number.	これが私の電話番号です。
	korega watashi no denwa bangoo desu
Call me.	電話してください。
	denwa shite kudasai
Text me.	携帯にメールを送ってください。
	keitai ni meeru o okutte kudasai
I'll call you.	電話します。
	denwa shimasu
I'll text you.	メールを送ります。
	meeru o okurimasu

YOU MAY HEAR...

どなたですか。	Who's calling?
donata desu ka	
少々お待ちください。	Hold on.
shoo shoo omachi kudasai	
おつなぎします。	I'll put you through.
otsunagi shimasu	
すみません。今、出ています。	I'm afraid he's/she's not in.
sumimasen ima dete imasu	
ただ今、電話に出られません。	He/She can't come to the phone.
tada ima denwa ni deraremasen	
ご伝言を承りましょうか。	Would you like to leave a message?
godengon o uketamawarimashoo ka	
後程/十分後にお電話ください。	Call back later/in 10 minutes.
nochihodo/juppungoni odenwa kudasai	
こちらからお電話いたしましょうか。	Can he/she call you back?
kochira kara odenwa itashimashoo ka	
お電話番号を頂けますか。	What's your number?
odenwa bangoo o itadakemasu ka	

You can find public phones in hotel lobbies, on the street and in train stations. You will be able to make overseas phone calls using coins, prepaid telephone cards purchased at a convenience store, or your credit card. Country codes: Canada and US are +1, UK is +44. Directory assistance in English: 0120-364-463 110 (police) or 119 (fire).

TELEPHONE ETIQUETTE

Hello. This is…	もしもし。…ですが。 *moshi moshi…desu ga*
I'd like to speak to…	…さん、お願いします。 *…san onegai shimasu*
Extension…	内線…番 *naisen…ban*
Speak louder/more slowly, please.	もう少し大きい声で/ゆっくりお願いします。 *mooo sukoshi ookii koe de/yukkuri onegai shimasu*
Could you repeat that, please?	もう一度、言ってください。 *moo ichido itte kudasai*
I'll call back later.	あとで電話します。 *atode denwa shimasu*
Bye.	ごめんください。 *gomen kudasai*

FAX

Can I send/receive a fax here?	ここでファックスを送れ/受け取れますか。 *kokode fakkusu o okure/uketore masu ka*
What's the fax number?	ファックスの番号を頂けますか。 *fakkusu no bangoo o itadakemasu ka*
Please fax this to…	これを…にファックスしてください。 *kore o…ni fakkusu shite kudasai*

POST

Where's the post office/mailbox [postbox]?	郵便局/郵便ポストはどこですか。 *yuubinkyoku/yuubin posuto wa doko desu ka*

Main post offices are open from 8:00 a.m. to 7:00 p.m. on weekdays, 9:00 a.m. to 5:00 p.m. on Saturdays and 9:00 a.m. to 12:30 p.m. on Sundays. Local post offices do not open on Sundays and will have limited hours mid-week. Tokyo International Post Office is open around the clock. Stamps are also sold at hotels and some tobacconists. Mailboxes, usually red, are found on street corners. You can also mail letters at hotels.

A stamp for this postcard/letter, please.	この葉書/手紙用の切手をください。 *kono hagaki/tegami yoo no kitte o kudasai*
How much?	いくらですか 。 *ikura desuka*
I want to send this package by airmail/express	この小包を速達/航空便で送りたいんですが。 *kono kozutsumi o sokutatsu/kookuubin de okuritain desu ga*
A receipt, please.	レシートをお願いします。 *reshiito o onegai shimasu*

YOU MAY HEAR...

税関申告書に記入してください。 *zeikan shinkokusho ni kinyuu shite kudasai*	Please fill out the customs declaration form.
どのくらいの値段のものですか。 *dono kurai no nedan no mono desu ka*	What's the value?
中には何が入っていますか。 *naka niwa nani ga haitte imasu ka*	What's inside?

SIGHTSEEING

NEED TO KNOW

Where's the tourist information office?	観光案内所はどこですか。
	kankoo annaijo wa doko desu ka
What are the main points of interest?	観光名所はどこですか。
	kankoo meesho wa doko desu ka
Do you have tours in English?	英語のツアーがありますか。
	eego no tsuaa ga arimasu ka
Could I have a map/guide please?	地図/案内書をください。
	chizu/annaisho o kudasai

TOURIST INFORMATION

Can you recommend...?	...はありますか。
	...wa arimasu ka
a boat trip	遊覧船
	yuuransen
an excursion	遊覧旅行
	yuuran ryokoo
a sightseeing tour	観光ツアー
	kankoo tsuaa
Do you have any information on...?	…の案内はありますか。
	...no annai wa arimasu ka

ON TOUR

I'd like to go on the tour to...	…へのツアーに参加したいんですが。
	...e no tsuaa ni sanka shitain desu ga
When's the next tour?	英語のツアーがありますか。
	sugi no tsuaa wa itsu desu ka

The Japan National Tourist Organization (JNTO) operates Tourist Information Centers (TIC) in Japan and overseas. These centers provide a wealth of information, including free maps, brochures, tour itineraries and advice on travel to and within Japan. They will give advice on the 'goodwill guide', a free service, as well as professional guide services.

In Tokyo, at Tokyo and Shinjuku rail stations, you will find special centers called Information for Foreigners (**gaikokujin annai jo**) providing foreigners with information on sightseeing, travel, living in Tokyo and much more.

Are there tours in English?	英語のツアーがありますか。 *eego no tsuaa ga arimasu ka*
Is there an English-speaking guide/audio guide?	英語のガイド/オーディオがありますか。 *eego no gaido/oodio ga arimasu ka*
What time do we leave/return?	何時に出ますか/戻りますか。 *nanji ni demasu ka/modorimasu ka*
We'd like to have a look at the...	…を見たいんですが。 *...o mitain desu ga*
Can we stop here...?	…ここで止まれますか。 *...koko de tomaremasu ka*
to take photographs	写真を撮りたいんですが、 *shashin o toritain desu ga*
to buy souvenirs	お土産を買いたいんですが、 *omiyage o kaitain desu ga*
to use the bathrooms [toilets]	トイレに行きたいんですが、 *toire ni ikitain desu ga*
Is there access for the disabled?	身体障害者は入れますか。 *shintai shogaisha wa hairemasu ka*

For Tickets, see page 47.

SEEING THE SIGHTS

Where is the...?	…はどこですか。
	…wa doko desu ka
art gallery	美術館
	bijutsukan
battle site	戦場跡
	senjoo ato
botanical garden	植物園
	shokubutsuen
Buddhist temple	お寺
	otera
castle	お城
	oshiro
castle remains	城跡
	shiro ato
cemetery	墓地
	bochi
church	教会
	kyookai
downtown area	繁華街
	hankagai
fountain	噴水
	funsui
historic site	史跡
	shiseki
(war) memorial	(戦争)記念碑
	(sensoo) kinen hi
museum	博物館
	hakubutsukan
five-story [storey]	五重塔
pagoda	*gojuu no too*
Imperial palace	皇居
	kookyo

Where is the...?	...はどこですか。	
	...wa doko desu ka	
park	公園	
	kooen	
parliament building	国会議事堂	
	kokkai gijidoo	
Shinto shrine	神社	
	jinja	
shopping area	商店街	
	shootengai	
statue	銅像	
	doozoo	
theater [theatre]	劇場	
	gekijoo	
town hall	市役所	
	shiyakusho	
Can you show me on the map?	この地図で教えてください。	
	kono chizu de oshiete kudasai	
It's...	...ですね。	
	...desu ne	
amazing	すごい	
	sugoi	
beautiful	美しい	
	utsukushii	
boring	つまらない	
	tsumaranai	
interesting	おもしろい	
	omoshiroi	
magnificent	立派	
	rippa	
romantic	ロマンチック	
	romanchikku	
strange	変	
	hen	

superb	素晴らしい
	subarashii
terrible	ひどい
	hidoi
ugly	醜い
	minikui

I like it./I don't like it. 好きです/好きではありません。
　　　　　　　　　　　suki desu/dewa arimasen

For Asking Directions, see page 65.

RELIGIOUS SITES

Where's…?	…はどこですか。
	…wa doko desu ka
the cathedral	大聖堂
	daiseedoo
the Catholic/	カトリック/プロテスタント教会
Protestant church	*katorikku/purotesutanto kyookai*
the mosque	回教寺院
	kaikyoo jiin
the Shinto shrine	神社
	jinja
the synagogue	ユダヤ教会堂
	yudaya kyookaidoo
the Buddhist/	寺/禅寺
Zen temple	*tera/zendera*
What time is mass/	ミサ / 礼拝 は何時ですか。
the service?	*misa/reehai wa nanji desu ka*

ACTIVITIES

SHOPPING

NEED TO KNOW

Where is the shopping center?	ショッピングセンターはどこですか。
	shoppinngu sentaa wa doko desu ka
I'm just looking.	ちょっと見ているだけです。
	chotto miteiru dake desu
Can you help me?	ちょっと, お願いします。
	chotto onegai shimasu
I'm being helped.	大丈夫です。
	daijoobu desu
How much?	いくらですか。
	ikura desu ka
That one.	それ
	sore
That's all, thanks.	それで結構です。
	sorede kekkoo desu
Where can I pay?	どこで払うんですか。
	doko de haraun desu ka
I'll pay in cash/by credit card.	現金/(クレジット)カードで払います。
	genkin/(kurejitto) kaado de haraimasu
A receipt, please.	レシートをお願いします。
	reshiito o onegai shimasu

AT THE SHOPS

Where's the...?	…はどこですか。
	...wa doko desu ka
antiques store	骨董品店
	kottoohinten

Japanese people usually shop at department stores for clothing and household items. You will not be able to bargain at department stores, which tend to sell more expensive items. There are two large, upscale shopping centers, Roppongi Hills and Omote Sando Hills, in Tokyo. If you want to find bargain items, visit a flea market at the neighborhood temple or town square, where vendors sell used kimonos, household items or antiques. If you are interested in small electronic items such as audio-video equipment, home appliances, computers, computer games or anime and anime related characters, visit Akihabara in Tokyo. Several blocks surrounding the Akihabara Station are filled with stores selling all kinds of items.

bakery	パン屋
	pan ya
bank	銀行
	ginkoo
bookstore	本屋
	hon ya

clothing store	洋服屋
	yoofukuya
delicatessen	デリカテッセン
	derikatessen
department store	デパート
	depaato
health food store	健康食品店
	kenkoo shokuhin ten
jeweler	宝石店
	hooseki ten
liquor store	酒屋
	sakaya
[off-licence]	
market	マーケット
	maaketto
pastry shop	ケーキ屋
	keekiya
pharmacy	薬局
[chemist]	*yakkyoku*
produce [grocery]	食料品店
store	*shokuryoohin ten*
shoe store	靴屋
	kutsuya
shopping mall	ショッピングセンター
[shopping centre]	*shoppinngu sentaa*
the souvenir store	お土産屋
	omiyageya
the supermarket	スーパー
	suupaa
the tobacconist	タバコ屋
	tabakoya
the toy store	おもちゃ屋
	omochaya

For Souvenirs, see page 119.

YOU MAY HEAR...

いらっしゃいませ。	Welcome!
irasshaimase	
少々お待ちください。	One moment.
shooshoo omachi kudasai	
何がよろしいですか。	What would you like?
nani ga yoroshii desu ka	
他に何かございますか。	Anything else?
hoka ni nanika gozaimasu ka	

ASK AN ASSISTANT

What are the opening hours?	開店時間は何時ですか。
	kaiten jikan wa nanji desu ka
Where is/are...?	…はどこですか。
	...wa doko desu ka
the cashier [cash desk]	会計
	kaikee
the escalator	エスカレーター
	esukareetaa
the elevator [lift]	エレベーター
	erebeetaa
the fitting room	試着室
	shichakushitsu
the store directory [guide]	店内の案内
	tennai no annai
Can you help me?	ちょっと、お願いします。
	chotto onegai shimasu
I'm just looking.	ちょっと見ているだけです。
	chotto miteiru dake desu
I'm being helped.	大丈夫です。
	daijoobu desu

Do you have…?	…は、ありますか。
	…wa arimasu ka
Could you show me…?	…を見せてください。
	…o misete kudasai
Can you ship/ wrap it?	届けて/包装してください。
	todokete/hoosoo shite kudasai
How much?	いくらですか。
	ikura desu ka
That's all, thanks.	それで全部です。
	sore de zenbu desu

For Clothing, see page 111.

YOU MAY SEE...

開店/閉店	open/closed
kaiten/heeten	
昼食のため休業中	closed for lunch
chuusyoku no tame kyuugyoo chuu	
試着室	fitting room
shichakushitsu	
お会計	cashier
okaikei	
現金のみ	cash only
genkin nomi	
クレジットカードも受け付けます	credit cards accepted
kurejitto kaado mo uketsuke masu	
営業時間	business hours
eigyoo jikan	
出口	exit
deguchi	

PERSONAL PREFERENCES

I'd like something…	…のが欲しいんですが。
	…no ga hoshiin desu ga
cheap/expensive	安い/高い
	yasui/takai
larger/smaller	もっと大きい/小さい
	motto ookii/chiisai
from this region	この地方から
	kono chihoo kara
Is it real?	本物ですか。
	honmono desu ka
Could you show me this/that?	これ/それを見せてください。
	kore/sore o misete kudasai
That's not quite what I want.	私が思っているのと少し違うんですが。
	watashi ga omotte iru noto sukoshi chigaun desu ga
No, I don't like it.	あまり好きではありません。
	amari suki dewa arimasen
That's too expensive.	高すぎます。
	taka sugimasu
I'd like to think about it.	考えさせてください。
	kangae sasete kudasai
I'll take it.	それにします。
	sore ni shimasu

PAYING & BARGAINING

How much?	いくらですか。
	ikura desu ka
I'll pay.	…で払います。
	…de haraimasu
in cash	現金
	genkin

YOU MAY HEAR...

お支払いはどうなさいますか。
oshiharai wa doo nasaimasu ka

このカードで承認が得られませんでした。
kono kaado de shoonin ga eraremasen deshita

他に身分証明はお持ちですか
hoka ni mibun shoomeisho wa omochi desu ka

現金でお願レ、します。
genkin de onegai shimasu

小銭はございますか。
kozeni wa gozaimasu ka

How are you paying?

This transaction has not been approved.

May I have additional identification?

Cash only, please.

Do you have any smaller change?

---

by credit card	(クレジット)カード
	(kurejitto) kaado
by traveler's check [cheque]	トラベラーズチェック
	toraberaazu chekku
A receipt, please.	レシートをお願いします。
	reshiito o onegai shimasu
That's too much.	高すぎます。
	taka sugimasu
I'll give you…	…でどうですか。
	…de doo desu ka
I only have…yen.	…円しかありません。
	…en shika arimasen
Is that your best price?	もっと安くなりませんか。
	motto yasuku narimasen ka
Can you give me a discount?	割引してくれませんか。
	waribiki shite kuremasen ka

ⓘ

Visitors to Japan can use the international credit
cards at most stores, however, withdrawing cash using
your credit card is limited to a small number of ATMs.

MAKING A COMPLAINT

I'd like...	…ですが 。
	...desu ga
to exchange this	交換したいん
	kookan shitain
to return this	返品したいん
	henpin shitain
a refund	返金してもらいたいん
	henkin shite moraitain
to see the manager	マネージャーに会いたいん
	maneejaa ni aitain

SERVICES

Can you recommend...?	いい…はありますか。
	ii...wa arimasu ka
a barber	床屋
	tokoya
a dry cleaner	ドライクリーニング店
	dorai kuriiningu ten
a hairdresser	美容院
	biyooin
a laundromat [launderette]	コインランドリー
	koin randorii
a nail salon	ネイルサロン
	neeru saron

a spa	スパ
	supa
a travel agency	旅行代理店
	ryokoo dairiten
Can you...this?	…できますか。
	...dekimasu ka
alter	仕立て直し
	shitatenaoshi
clean	洗濯
	sentaku
mend	修繕
	shuuzen
press	プレス
	puresu
When will it be ready?	いつできますか。
	itsu dekimasu ka

For Days, see page 26.

HAIR & BEAUTY

I'd like...	…をお願いしたいんですが。
	...o onegaishitain desu ga
an appointment for today/tomorrow	今日/明日の予約
	kyoo/ashita no yoyaku
some color	カラー
	karaa
some highlights	ハイライト
	hairaito
my hair styled	スタイル
	sutairu
a haircut	カット
	katto

I'd like a trim.	そろえてもらいたいんですが。	
	soroete moraitain desu ga	
Don't cut it too short.	切りすぎないでください。	
	kiri suginai de kudasai	
Shorter here.	ここをもう少し短くして下さい。	
	koko o moo sukoshi mijikaku shite kudasai	
I'd like.	...をお願いしたいんですが。	
	...o onegai shitain desuga	
an eyebrow/bikini wax	眉毛/ビキニワックス	
	mayuge/bikini wakkusu	
a facial	フエーシヤノレ	
	feesharu	
a manicure	マニキュア	
	manikyua	
pedicure	ペディキュア	
	pedikyua	
a (sports) massage	(スポーツ)マッサージ	
	supootsu massaaji	
Do you do...?	...をしますか。	
	...o shimasu ka	
acupuncture	鍼	
	hari	
aromatherapy	アロマセラピー	
	aromaserapii	

> ⓘ
>
> For relaxation in a traditional setting, visit one of many hot springs throughout Japan. You will find special facilities at hotels and Japanese inns near hot spring areas. A hot spring is enjoyed just like a bath: traditionally no bathing suit is worn, and there are separate areas for men and women. Sometimes you will find a smaller area for family use. In addition to the hot springs, there are many day spas in the cities, and hotel and resort spas are also available. Prices are comparable to the west, but tipping is not expected.

oxygen treatment	酸素治療
	sanso chiryoo
Is there a sauna?	サウナがありますか。
	sauna ga arimasu ka

For Pharmacy, see page 149.

ANTIQUES

How old is this?	どのくらい古いですか。
	dono kurai furui desu ka
Do you have anything of the…era?	…時代のものはありますか。
	…jidai no mono wa arimasu ka
Will I have problems with customs?	税関で問題になりますか。
	zeekan de mondai ni narimasu ka
Is there a certificate of authenticity?	鑑定書はありますか。
	kanteesho wa arimasu ka

For Souvenirs, see page 119.

CLOTHING

I'd like.	…が欲しいんですが。 *…ga hoshiin desu ga*
Can I try this on?	これを試着できますか。 *kore o shichaku dekimasu ka*
It doesn't fit.	身体に合いません。 *karada ni aimasen*
It's too…	…すぎます。 *…sugimasu*
big	大き *ooki*
small	小さ *chiisa*
short	短 *mijika*
long	長 *naga*
Do you have this in size…?	これで…サイズのはありますか。 *korede… saizu no wa arimasu ka*
Do you have this in a bigger/smaller size?	もう少し大きい/小さいのがありますか。 *moo sukoshi ookii/chiisai no ga arimasu ka*

For Numbers, see page 20.

YOU MAY SEE…

紳士服	men's clothing
婦人服	women's clothing
子供服	children's clothing

YOU MAY HEAR…

とてもよくお似合いです。
totemo yoku oniai desu
いかがですか。
ikaga desu ka
お客様に合うサイズがありません。
okyaku sama ni au saizu ga arima sen

That looks
great on you.
How does it fit?

We don't have
your size.

COLORS

I'm looking for something in…	…のを探しているんですが。
	…no o sagashite irun desu ga
beige	ベージュ
	beeju
black	黒い
	kuroi
blue	ブルー
	buruu
brown	茶色
	chairo
green	グリーン
	guriin
gray [grey]	グレー
	guree
orange	オレンジ色
	orenji iro
pink	ピンク
	pinku
purple	紫
	murasaki
red	赤い
	akai

white	白い
	shiroi
yellow	黄色
	kiiro

CLOTHES & ACCESSORIES

backpack	リュックサック
	ryukkusakku
belt	ベルト
	beruto
bikini	ビキニ
	bikini
blouse	ブラウス
	burausu
bra	ブラジャー
	burajaa
coat	コート
	kooto
dress	ワンピース
	wanpiisu
hat	帽子
	booshi
jacket	上着
	uwagi
jeans	ジーパン
	jiipan
pajamas	パジャマ
	pajama
panties	パンティー（女性用の下着）
(women's underwear)	*pantii (joseiyoo no shitagi)*
pants [trousers]	ズボン
	zubon

panty hose [tights]	パンスト
	pansuto
purse [handbag]	ハンドバッグ
	handobaggu
raincoat	レインコート
	einkooto
scarf	スカーフ
	sukaafu
shirt (men's)	ワイシャツ
	waishatsu
shorts	半ズボン
	hanzubon
skirt	スカート
	sukaato
socks	靴下
	kutsushita
suit	スーツ
	suutsu
sunglasses	サングラス
	sangurasu
sweater	セーター
	seetaa
sweatshirt	トレーナー
	toreenaa
swimsuit	水着
	mizugi
T-shirt	Tシャツ
	tii shatsu
tie	ネクタイ
	nekutai
underpants	ノベンツ
	pantsu

FABRIC

I'd like...	...が欲しいんですが。
	...ga hoshiin desu ga
cotton	綿/コットン
	men/kotton
denim	デニム
	denimu
lace	レース
	reesu
leather	革
	kawa
linen	麻
	asa
silk	絹
	kinu
wool	ウール
	uuru
Is it machine washable?	洗濯機で洗えますか。
	sentakuki de araemasu ka

SHOES

I'd like...	...が欲しいんですが 。
	...ga hoshiin desu ga
high-heeled/flat shoes.	ハイヒール/平らな靴
	haihiiru/taira na kutsu
boots	ブーツ
	buutsu
loafers	ローファー
	roofaa
sandals	サンダル
	sandaru

shoes	靴
	kutsu
slippers	スリッパ
	surippa
sneakers	スニーカー
	suniikaa
In size…	サイズ…の
	saizu…no

SIZES

small (S)	小
	shoo
medium (M)	中
	chuu
large (L)	大
	dai
extra large (XL)	特大
	tokudai
petite	プチサイズ
	puchi saizu
plus size	大きいサイズ
	ookii saizu

i

In Friendship stores and places where clothes are made for export, sizes will be given as small, medium and large. Most other clothing stores feature Chinese measurements that combine height and chest size; these measurements appear in centimeters. For example, if you are 170 cm tall (5'6") with a chest measurement of 90 cm (36"), look for clothing marked 170/90. Children's sizes are given by height, in centimeters.

NEWSAGENT & TOBACCONIST

Do you sell English-language books/ newspapers?	英語の本/新聞はありますか。 *eego no hon/shinbun wa arimasu ka*	
I'd like…	…が欲しいんですが。 *…ga hoshiin desu ga*	
candy [sweets]	キャンデー *kyandee*	
chewing gum	ガム *gamu*	
a chocolate bar	チョコレート *chokoreeto*	
cigars	葉巻 *hamaki*	
a pack/carton of cigarettes	煙草一箱/一カートン *tabako hitohako/ichi kaaton*	
a lighter	ライター *raitaa*	
a magazine	雑誌 *zasshi*	

matches	マッチ
	matchi
a newspaper	新聞
	shinbun
a pen	ボールペン
	boorupen
a postcard	絵葉書
	ehagaki
a road/town map of...	…の道路/市街地図
	...no dooro/shigai chizu
stamps	切手
	kitte

PHOTOGRAPHY

I'm looking for a(n)...camera.	…カメラを探しているんですが。
	...kamera o sagashite irun desu ga
automatic	オートマチック
	ootomachikku
digital	デジタル
	dejitaru
disposable	使い捨て
	tsukaisute
I'd like...	…が欲しいんですが。
	...ga hoshiin desu ga
a battery	電池
	denchi
digital prints	デジタルカメラプリント
	dejitaru kamera purinto
a memory card	メモリーカード
	memorii kaado
Can I print digital photos here?	デジタル写真をプリントできますか。
	dejitaru shashin o purinto dekimasu ka

SOUVENIRS

dolls	人形	
	ningyoo	
electrical goods	電気製品	
	denki seehin	
fans	扇子	
	sensu	
cloth wrap traditionally used as a handbag	風呂敷 *furoshiki*	
handcrafts	工芸品	
	koogeehin	
kimono	着物	
	kimono	
lacquerware	漆器	
	shikki	
ornaments	装飾品	
	sooshokuhin	
paper crafts	紙細工	
	kami zaiku	
pearls	真珠	
	shinju	
porcelain	磁器	
	jiki	
pottery	焼き物	
	yakimono	
prints	版画	
	hanga	
sake (rice wine)	日本酒	
	nihonshu	
woodblock prints	木版	
	mokuhan	

yukata (cotton bathrobe)	浴衣 *yukata*
Can I see this/that?	これ/それをお願いします。 *kore/sore o onegai shimasu*
It's the one in the window/display case.	ショーウインドー/ケースにあるのです。 *shoouindoo/keesu ni aru no desu*
I'd like.	…が欲しいんですが。 *…ga hoshiin desu ga*
a battery	電池 *denchi*
a bracelet	ブレスレット *buresuretto*
a brooch	ブローチ *buroochi*
earrings	イヤリング *iyaringu*
a necklace	ネックレス *nekkuresu*
a ring	指輪/リング *yubiwa/ringu*
a watch	腕時計 *ude dokee*
I'd like…	…が欲しいんですが。 *…ga hoshiin desu ga*
copper	銅 *doo*
crystal (quartz)	水晶 *suishoo*
diamonds	ダイアモンド *daiamondo*
white/yellow gold	プラチナ/金 *purachina/kin*

pearls	真珠 *shinju*
pewter	ピューター *pyuutaa*
platinum	プラチナ *purachina*
sterling silver	純銀 *jungin*
Is this real?	本物ですか。 *honmono desu ka*
Can you engrave it?	…を彫り込んでください。 *…o horikonde kudasai*

You will have no difficulty finding any number of souvenirs and presents to take home. There is something for everybody and in every price range. If you are buying electrical goods, remember that Japan uses 100 volts and that television/video systems may not be compatible. Different regions have their own specialties: you'll find pottery in Mashiko (north of Tokyo), **Bizen** (a specific type of pottery) in Okayama and lacquer-ware (called **shikki**) in Aizu (in Fukushima prefecture), Wajima (in Ishikawa prefecture) and Hida Takayama (in Gifu prefecture). You may also be interested in bamboo products, which are produced throughout Japan.

SPORT & LEISURE

NEED TO KNOW

When's the game?	試合はいつですか。
	shiai wa itsu desu ka
Where's…?	…はどこですか。
	…wa doko desu ka
the beach	ビーチ
	biichi
the park	公園
	kooen
the pool	プール
	puuru
Is it safe to swim/ dive here?	ここで泳いでも/飛び込んでも大丈夫 ですか。
	kokode oyoidemo/tobikondemo daijoobu desu ka
Can I rent [hire] golf clubs?	ゴルフクラブを借りたいんですが。
	gorufu kurabu o karitain desu ga
How much per hour?	料金は1時間いくらですか。
	ryookin wa ichijikan ikura desu ka
How much per round? (when hiring court)	1試合につきいくらですか。
	hitoshiai ni tsuki ikura desuka
How far is it to…?	…まで、どのくらいありますか。
	…made dono kurai arimasu ka
Can you show me on the map?	この地図で教えてください。
	kono chizu de oshiete kudasai

WATCHING SPORT

When's...?	...はいつですか。
	...wa itsu desu ka
the basketball game	バスケットボール
	basuketto booru no shiai
the baseball game	野球の試合
	yakyuu no shiai
the boxing match	ボクシングの試合
	bokushingu no shiai
the cycling race	自転車レース
	jitensha reesu
the golf tournament	ゴノレフトーナメント
	gorufu toonamento
the soccer game	サッカーの試合
	sakkaa no shiai
the tennis match	テニスの試合
	tenisu no shiai
the volleyball game	バレーボールの試合
	bareebooru no shiai
Which teams are playing?	どのチームが出ますか。
	dono chiimu ga demasu ka
Where's...?	...はどこですか。
	...wa doko desu ka

Most sports that are popular in the West — such as golf, tennis, football, basketball, etc. — are also popular in Japan. Many cities have martial arts halls in which you can watch **kendoo**, **juudoo**, **aikidoo** and **karate**. Japan's real national sport is **sumoo** (wrestling). This is an ancient, highly ritualized sport providing a true spectacle. There are six tournaments a year, each lasting 15 days. These are held in January, May, and September in Tokyo; in March in Osaka; July in Nagoya; November in Fukuoka. Skiing is also very popular in this mountainous country, and there are numerous ski resorts. It is best to reserve ski accommodations before you leave.

the horsetrack	競馬場	
	keebajoo	
the racetrack	競馬場	
	keebajoo	
the stadium	スタジアム	
	sutajiamu	
Where can I place a bet?	どこで賭け金を払いますか。	
	doko de kakekin o haraimasu ka	

PLAYING SPORT

Where's...?	…はどこですか。	
	…wa doko desu ka	
the golf course	ゴルフ場	
	gorufujoo	
the gym	スポーツジム	
	supootsu jimu	
the park	公園	
	kooen	

the tennis courts	テニスコート
	tenisu kooto
How much per…	料金は
	…いくらですか。
	ryookin wa …ikura desu ka
day	日
	nichi/hi
hour	時間
	jikan
game	試合
	shiai
round	ラウンド
	raundo
Can I rent [hire]…?	…を借りられますか。
	…o kariraremasu ka
golf clubs	クラブ
	kurabu
equipment	道具
	doogu
a racket	ラケット
	raketto

AT THE BEACH/POOL

Where's the beach/pool?	ビーチ/プールはどこですか。
	biichi/puuru wa doko desu ka
Is there…?	…はありますか。
	…wa arimasu ka
a kiddie pool	子供用のプール
	kodomo yoo no puuru
an indoor/outdoor pool	屋内/屋外プール
	okunai/okugai puuru
a lifeguard	プール監視員
	puuru kanshiin

Is it safe...?	...大丈夫ですか。
	...daijoobu desu ka
to swim	泳いでも
	oyoidemo
to dive	飛び込んでも
	tobikondemo
for children	子供に
	kodomo ni
I want to rent [hire]...	...を借りたいんですが。
	...o karitain desu ga
a deck chair	デッキチェア
	dekki chea
diving equipment	スキューバダイビング用具
	sukyuuba daibingu yoogu
a jet-ski	ジェットスキー
	jetto sukii
a motorboat	モーターボート
	mootaa booto
a rowboat	ボート
	booto
snorkeling equipment	シュノーケル
	shunookeru
a surfboard	サーフボード
	saafuboodo
a towel	タオル
	taoru

Beaches close to Tokyo and Osaka can be very crowded in the summer, and until September 1, when summer officially ends. Okinawa, the Amakusa Islands, the Yaeyama Islands are good for snorkeling and scuba diving.

an umbrella	パラソル
	parasoru
water skis	水上スキー
	suijoo sukii
a windsurfer	ウインドサーフィン
	uindo saafin
For...hours.	…時間
	...jikan

WINTER SPORTS

A lift pass for a day/ five days, please.	一日/五日分のリフト券、お願いします。
	ichinichi/itsuka bun no rifutoken onegai shimasu
I want to rent [hire]...	…を借りたいんですが。
	...o karitain desu ga
boots	スキー靴
	sukii gutsu
a helmet	ヘルメット
	herumetto
poles	ストック
	sutokku
skis	スキー
	sukii

a snowboard	スノーボード
	sunoo boodo
snowshoes	スノーシューズ
	sunooshuuzu
These are too big/small.	大き/小さすぎます。
	ooki/chiisa sugimasu
Are there lessons?	レッスンがありますか
	ressun ga arimasu ka
I'm a beginner.	初心者です。
	shoshinsha desu
I'm experienced.	経験者です。
	keekensha desu
A trail [piste] map, please.	ゲレンデマップ、お願いします。
	gerende mappu onegai shimasu

YOU MAY SEE...

ケーブルカー	cable car
リフト	chair lift
初心者	novice
中級	intermediate
上級	expert
コーズ閉鎖中	trail [piste] closed

You will find opportunities for both downhill and cross-country skiing in Japan. Many travelers choose to combine skiing with the delights of a **ryokan** or **minshuku** (traditional Japanese guest houses) offering a hot spa.

bridge	橋
	hashi
cave	洞窟
	dookutsu
canal	運河
	unga
cliff	崖
	gake
farmhouse	農家
	nooka
field	野原
	nohara
forest	森
	mori
hill	丘
	oka
island	島
	shima
lake	湖
	mizuumi
mountain	山
	yama
mountain pass	山道
	yama michi
mountain range	山脈
	sanmyaku
nature reserve	自然保護区域
	shizen hogo kuiki
panorama	展望
	tenboo
park	公園
	kooen
peak	山頂
	sanchoo

OUT IN THE COUNTRY

I'd like a map of…	…の地図をください。
	…no chizu o kudasai
this region	この地域
	kono chiiki
the walking routes	ハイキングコース
	haikingu koosu
bike routes	サイクリングコース
	saikuringu koosu
the trails	ハイキング
	haikingu
Is it easy/difficult?	やさしい/難しいですか。
	yasashii/muzukashii desu ka
Is it far/steep?	遠い/急斜面ですか。
	tooi/kyuushamen desu ka
How far is it to…?	…まで、どのくらいありますか。
	…made dono kurai arimasu ka
Can you show me on the map?	この地図で教えてください。
	kono chizu de oshiete kudasai
I'm lost.	道に迷いました。
	michi ni mayoimashita
Where's the…?	…はどこですか。
	…wa doko desu ka

plain	平野
	heeya
pond	池
	ike
rapids	急流
	kyuuryuu
river	川
	kawa
hot spring	温泉
	onsen
stream	小川
	ogawa
valley	谷間
	tanima
viewpoint	展望台
	tenboo dai
village	村
	mura
waterfall	滝
	taki
wood	林
	hayashi

NEED TO KNOW

Is there a discount for children?	子供の割引はありますか。
	kodomo no waribiki wa arimasu ka
Can you recommend a baby sitter?	信頼できるベビーシッターを教えてください。
	shinrai dekiru bebii shittaa o oshiete kudasai
Could we have a child's seat/ highchair?	子供用の椅子/ハイチェアをお願いします。
	kodomo yoo no isu/hai chea o onegai shimasu
Where can I change the baby?	おむつはどこで替えられますか。
	omutsu wa doko de kaeraremasu ka

OUT & ABOUT

Can you recommend something for the kids?	子供が楽しめるところを教えてください。
	kodomo ga tanoshimeru tokoro o oshiete kudasai
Where's...?	…はどこですか
	...wa doko desu ka
the amusement park	遊園地
	yuuenchi
the arcade	ゲームセンター
	geemu sentaa
the kiddie [paddling] pool	子供用のプール
	kodomo yoo no puuru
the playground	公園
	kooen
the zoo	動物園
	doobutsu en
Are kids allowed?	子供でも入れますか。
	kodomo demo hairemasu ka
Is it safe for kids?	子供でも大丈夫ですか。
	kodomo demo daijoobu desu ka
Is it suitable for... year olds?	…歳の子供でも大丈夫ですか。
	...sai no kodomo demo daijoobu desu ka

BABY ESSENTIALS

Do you have...?	…は、ありますか。
	...wa arimasu ka
a baby bottle	哺乳瓶
	honyuubin
baby wipes	お尻拭き
	oshiri fuki
a car seat	チャイルドシート
	chairudo shiito

a children's menu	お子さまメニュー
	okosama menyuu
a child's seat/ highchair	子供用のイス/ハイチェア
	kodomo yoo no isu/haichea
a crib	ベビーベッド
	bebii beddo
diapers [nappies]	(紙)おむつ
	(kami) omutsu
formula	ミルク
	miruku
a pacifier [soother]	おしゃぶり
	oshaburi
a playpen	ベビーサークル
	bebii saakuru
a stroller [pushchair]	ベビーカー
	bebiikaa
Can I breastfeed the baby here?	ここで授乳してもいいですか。
	kokode junyuu shitemo ii desu ka
Where can I change the baby?	おむつはどこで替えられますか。
	omutsu wa doko de kaeraremasu ka

YOU MAY HEAR...

かわいい!
kawaii
How cute!

お名前は?
onamae wa
What's his/her name?

何歳ですか。
nansai desu ka
How old is he/she?

BABYSITTING

Can you recommend a reliable baby sitter?	信頼できるベビーシッターを教えてください。
	shinrai dekiru bebii shittaa o oshiete kudasai
What's the charge?	料金 はいくらですか。
	ryookin wa ikura desu ka
I'll pick them up at...	…に迎えに 行きます。
	...ni mukae ni ikimasu
I can be reached at...	…に電話してください。
	...ni denwa shite Kudasai

For Time, see page 25.

HEALTH & SAFETY

EMERGENCIES

NEED TO KNOW

Help!	助けて! *tasukete*
Go away!	あっちへ行け! *atchi e ike*
Call the police!	警察を呼んで! *keesatsu o yonde*
Stop thief!	泥棒! *doroboo*
Get a doctor!	医者を呼んで! *isha o yonde*
Fire!	火事だ! *kaji da*
I'm lost.	道に迷いました。 *michi ni mayoimashita*
Can you help me?	助けてください。 *tasukete kudasai*

In an emergency, dial: **110** for the police;
119 for the fire brigade and emergency medical services.

YOU MAY HEAR...

この用紙に記入してください。
kono yooshi ni kinyuu shite kudasai
身分証明書を見せてください。
mibun shoomeisho o misete kudasai

いつ/どこで起きたんですか。
itsu/dokode okitan desu ka
どんな顔をしていますか。
donna kao o shite iamsu ka

Please fill out
this form.
Your
identification,
please.
When/Where
did it happen?
What does he/
she look like?

POLICE

NEED TO KNOW

Call the police!	警察を呼んで！
	keesatsu o yonde
Where's the police station?	交番はどこですか。
	kooban wa doko desu ka
There has been an accident/attack.	事故がありました/襲われました。
	jiko ga arimashita/osowaremashita
My child is missing.	子供がいなくなりました。
	kodomo ga inaku narimashita
I need an interpreter.	通訳が要るんですが。
	tsuuyaku ga irun desu ga
I need...	…したいんですが。
	...shitain desu ga
to contact my lawyer	弁護士に連絡
	bengoshi ni renraku
to make a phonecall	電話
	denwa
I'm innocent.	無実です。
	mujitsu desu

CRIME & LOST PROPERTY

I want to report...	…を報告したいんですが。
	...o hookoku shitaindesu ga
a mugging	強盗
	gootoo
a rape	レイプ
	reepu

a theft	泥棒	
	doroboo	
I've been mugged.	強盗にあいました。	
	gootoo ni aimashita	
I've lost my...	…をなくしました。	
	...o nakushimashita	
My...has been stolen	….を盗まれました。	
	...o nusumaremashita	
backpack	リュックサック	
	ryukkusakku	
bicycle	自転車	
	jitensha	
camera	カメラ	
	kamera	
car	車	
	kuruma	
rental car	レンタカー	
	renta kaa	
computer	コンピュータ	
	konpyuuta	
credit cards	クレジットカード	
	kurejitto kaado	
jewelry	宝石	
	hooseki	
money	お金	
	okane	
passport	パスポート	
	pasupooto	
purse/wallet	財布	
	saifu	
traveler's checks [cheques]	トラベラーズチェック	
	toraberaazu chekku	

I need a police report for my insurance claim. 保険の申請に警察の証明書が要ります。
hoken no shinsee ni keesatsu no shoomeesho ga irimasu

Where is the British/American/Irish embassy? 英国/アメリカ/アイルランド大使館はどこですか。
eikoku/amerika/airurando taishikan wa doko desu ka

I need an interpreter. 通訳が必要です。
tsuuyaku ga hitsuyoo desu

HEALTH

NEED TO KNOW

I'm sick. 具合が悪いんです。
guai ga waruin desu

I need an English-speaking doctor. 英語ができる医者はいますか。
eego ga dekiru isha wa imasu ka

It hurts here. ここが痛いんです。
koko ga itain desu

I have a stomachache. お腹が痛いんです。
onaka ga itain desu

FINDING A DOCTOR

Can you recommend a doctor/dentist? 医者/歯医者を教えてください。
isha/haisha o oshiete kudasai

Could the doctor come to see me here? 往診してくれますか。
ooshin shite kuremasu ka

I need an English-speaking doctor.	英語ができる医者はいますか。
	eego ga dekiru isha wa imasu ka
What are the office hours?	診察時間はいつですか。
	shinsatsu jikan wa itsu desu ka
Can I make an appointment…?	…予約したいんですが。
	…yoyaku shitain desu ga
for today	今日
	kyoo
for tomorrow	明日
	ashita
as soon as possible	できるだけ早く
	dekirudake hayaku
It's urgent.	至急お願いします。
	shikyuu onegai shimasu

SYMPTOMS

I'm…	しています。
	shite imasu
bleeding	出血
	shukketsu
constipated	便秘
	benpi
dizzy	目眩
	memai
It hurts here.	ここが痛いんです。
	koko ga itai n desu
I'm nauseous/vomiting.	吐きそうです/吐いています。
	hakisoo desu/haite imasu
I have…	…があります。
	…ga arimasu
an allergic reaction	アレルギー反応
	arerugii hannoo

chest pain	胸の痛み *mune no itami*
an earache	耳の痛み *mimi no itami*
a fever	熱 *netsu*
pain	痛み *itami*
a rash	発疹 *hasshin*
some swelling	腫れ *hare*

YOU MAY HEAR...

どうしましたか。 *doo shimashita ka*	What's wrong?
どこが痛みますか。 *doko ga itamimasu ka*	Where does it hurt?
ここが痛みますか。 *koko ga itamimasu ka*	Does it hurt here?
他に薬を飲んでいますか。 *hokani kusuri o nonde imasu ka*	Are you taking any other medication?
何かのアレルギーはありますか。 *nanka no arerugii wa arimasu ka*	Are you allergic to anything?
口を開けてください。 *kuchi o akete kudasai*	Open your mouth.
深呼吸してください。 *shin kokyuu shite kudasai*	Breathe deeply.
病院に行ってください。 *byooin ni itte kudasai*	Please go to the hospital.

I have a sprain.	ねんざしました。
	nenza shimashita
I have a	お腹が痛いんです。
stomachache.	*onaka ga itain desu*
I have sunstroke.	日射病にかかりました。
	nisshabyoo ni kakarimashita
I've been sick for...	…日間, 病気です。
days	*...nichikan byooki desu*

CONDITIONS

I'm.	…です。
	...desu
anemic	貧血症
	hinketsu shoo
asthmatic	ぜんそく
	zensoku
diabetic	糖尿病
	toonyoo byoo
epileptic	てんかん症
	tenkanshoo

I'm allergic to antibiotics/penicillin.	抗生物質/ペニシリンにアレルギーがあります。
	koosei busshitsu/penishirin ni arerugii ga arimasu
I have arthritis.	関節炎にかかっています。
	kansetsuen ni kakatte imasu
I have (high/low) blood pressure.	高/低血圧です。
	koo/tei ketsuatsu desu
I have a heart condition.	心臓が悪いんです。
	shinzoo ga waruin desu
I'm on…	…を飲んでいます。
	…o nonde imasu
I'm …months pregnant.	妊娠…ヶ月です。
	ninshin … ka getsu desu

TREATMENT

Do I need a prescription/medicine?	処方箋/薬が必要ですか。
	shohoo sen/kusuri ga hitsuyoo desu ka
Can you prescribe a generic drug [unbranded medication]?	後発医薬品を処方してもらえますか。
	koohatsu iyakuhin o shohoo shite morae masu ka

Where can I get it?	どこで買えますか。
	doko de kae masu ka

For What to Take, see page 150.

HOSPITAL

Please notify my family.	家族に知らせてください。
	kazoku ni shirasete kudasai
I'm in pain.	痛みます。
	itamimasu
I need a doctor/ nurse.	医者/看護師を呼んでください。
	isha/kangoshi o yonde kudasai
When are visiting hours?	面会時間はいつですか。
	menkai jikan wa itsu desu ka
I'm visiting.	…の見舞いに来ました。
	…no mimai ni kimashita

DENTIST

I've broken a tooth/ lost a filling.	歯を折りました/詰め物をなくしました。
	ha o orimashita/tsumemono o nakushimashita
I have a toothache.	歯が痛いんです。
	ha ga itain desu
Can you fix this denture?	この入れ歯を直せますか。
	kono ireba o naosemasu ka

GYNECOLOGIST

I have menstrual cramps/a vaginal infection.	生理痛/膣感染症があります。
	seeritsuu/chitsu kansen shoo ga arimasu
I missed my period.	生理がありませんでした。
	seeri ga arimasen deshita

I'm on the Pill.	ピルを飲んでいます。
	piru o nonde imasu
I'm pregnant/not pregnant.	妊娠しています/いません。
	ninshin shite imasu/imasen
I haven't had my period for...months.	生理が…ヶ月間ありません。
	seeri ga... kagetsukan arimasen

OPTICIAN

I've lost.	…をなくしました。
	...o nakushimashita
one of my contact lenses	片方のコンタクトレンズ
	katahoo no kontakuto renzu
my glasses	眼鏡
	megane
a lens	レンズ
	renzu

PAYMENT & INSURANCE

How much?	いくらですか。
	ikura desuka
Can I pay by credit card?	クレジットカードを使えますか。
	kurejitto kaado o tsukaemasu ka
I have insurance.	保険に入っています。
	hoken ni haitte imasu
Can I have a receipt for my insurance?	保険申請のためにレシートをください。
	hoken shinsee no tame ni reshiito o kudasai

PHARMACY

NEED TO KNOW

Where's the nearest (all-night) pharmacy?
(夜間営業の)薬局はどこですか。
(yakan eegyoo no) yakkyoku wa doko desu ka

What time does the pharmacy open/close?
薬局は何時に開き/閉まりますか。
yakkyoku wa nanji ni aki/shimari masu ka

What would you recommend for...?
…には何がいいですか。
...niwa nani ga ii desu ka

How much should I take?
どのくらい飲むんですか。
dono kurai nomun desu ka

Can you fill [makeup] this prescription for me?
この薬をください。
kono kusuri o kudasai

I'm allergic to...
私は…にアレルギーがあります。
watashi wa... ni arerugii ga arimasu

ⓘ

You will find a large selection of imported medications at the American Pharmacy in Tokyo. These can be more expensive than at home, so if you have any special medical needs it is best to bring an ample supply with you.

WHAT TO TAKE

How much should I take?	どのくらい飲むんですか。 *dono kurai nomun desu ka*
How many times a day should I take it?	一日何回飲むんですか。 *ichinichi nankai nomun desu ka*
Is it suitable for children?	子供でも飲めますか。 *kodomo demo nomemasu ka*
I'm taking…	…を飲んでいます。 *…o nonde imasu*
Are there side effects?	副作用はありますか。 *fukusayoo wa arimasu ka*
I'd like some medicine for…	…の薬をください。 *…no kusuri o kudasai*
a cold	風邪 *kaze*
a cough	咳 *seki*
diarrhea	下痢 *geri*
a headache	頭痛 *zutsuu*
a toothache	歯が痛い *haga itai*
I'd like some medicine for…	…の薬をください。 *…no kusuri o kudasai*

insect bites	虫刺され
	mushi sasare
motion [travel] sickness	乗物酔い
	norimono yoi
a sore throat	喉の痛み
	nodo no itami
sunburn	日焼け
	hiyake
an upset stomach	胃痛
	itsuu

YOU MAY SEE...

一日一回／三回	once/three times a day
錠	tablet(s)
滴	drop
ティースプーン／茶さじ	teaspoon(s)
食前／食後／食間	before/after/in between meals
空腹時	on an empty stomach
丸ごと飲み下し	swallow whole
眠気を催すことがあります	may cause drowsniness
外用薬	for external use only

BASIC SUPPLIES

I'd like...	…が欲しいんですが 。
	...ga hoshiin desu ga
acetaminophen	アセタミノーフェン
[paracetamol]	*asetaminoofen*
antiseptic cream	傷薬
	kizugusuri
aspirin	頭痛薬
	zutsuuyaku
bandages	包帯
	hootai
a comb	櫛
	kushi
condoms	コンドーム
	kondoomu
contact lens	コンタクトレンズ液
solution	*kontakutorenzu eki*
deodorant	デオドラント
	deodoranto
a hairbrush	ヘアブラシ
	heaburashi
hair spray	ヘアスプレー
	hea supuree
ibuprofen	イブプロフェン
	ibupuroren
insect repellent	防虫剤
	boochuuzai
a nail file	ネイルファイル
	neirufairu
a (disposable)	(使い捨て) カミソリ
razor	*(tsukaisuite) kamisori*
razor blades	カミソリの刃
	kamisori no ha

sanitary napkins [pads]	生理用ナプキン
	seeri yoo napukin
shampoo/ conditioner	シャンプー/コンディショナー
	shanpuu/kondishonaa
soap	石鹸
	sekken
sunscreen	日焼け止めクリーム
	hiyake dome kuriimu
tampons	タンポン
	tanpon
tissues	ティッシュペーパー
	tisshu peepaa
toilet paper	トイレットペーパー
	toiretto peepaa
toothpaste	歯磨き粉
	hamigakiko

For Baby Essentials, see page 133.

CHILD HEALTH & EMERGENCY

Can you recommend a pediatrician?	小児科医を教えてください。
	shoonikai o oshiete kudasai
My child is allergic to...	うちの子供は…にアレルギーがあります。
	uchi no kodomo wa…ni arerugii ga arimasu
My child is missing.	子供がいなくなりました。
	kodomo ga inaku narimashita
Have you seen a boy/girl?	男/女の子を見ましたか。
	otoko/onna no ko o mimashita ka

For Police, see page 140.

DISABLED TRAVELERS

NEED TO KNOW

Is there...?	…はありますか。
	...wa arimasu ka
access for the disabled	身体障害者用通路
	shintai shogaisha yoo tsuuro
a wheelchair ramp	車椅子用スロープ
	kuruma isu yoo suroopu
a handicapped [disabled] accessible toilet	ハンディキャップ用トイレ
	handikyappu yoo toire
I need...	… が要るんですが。
	...ga irun desu ga
assistance	助け
	tasuke
an elevator [lift]	エレベーター
	erebeetaa
a ground floor room	1階の部屋
	ikkai no heya

Many provincial main stations have elevators and other facilities for disabled travelers. However, smaller stations generally do not.

ASKING FOR ASSISTANCE

I'm disabled.	私は身体が不自由です。
	watashi wa karada ga fujiyuu desu
I'm deaf.	私は耳が聞こえません。
	watashi wa mimi ga kikoemasen
I'm visually/hearing impaired.	私は目がよく見えません/耳がよく聞こえません。
	watashi wa me ga yoku miemasen/mimi ga yoku kikoemasen
I'm unable to walk far/use the stairs.	私は遠くまで歩けません/階段を上れません。
	watashi wa tooku made arukemasen/ kaidan o noboremasen
Can I bring my wheelchair?	車椅子を持っていってもいいですか。
	kurumaisu o motte ittemo ii desu ka
Are guide dogs permitted?	盲導犬が入ってもいいですか。
	moodooken ga haittemo ii desu ka
Can you help me?	助けてください。
	tasukete kudasai
Please open/hold the door.	ドアを開けて/開けておいてください。
	doa o akete/akete oite kudasai

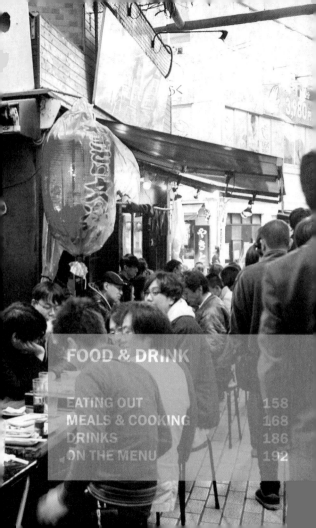

FOOD & DRINK

EATING OUT

NEED TO KNOW

Can you recommend a good restaurant/bar?	いいレストラン/バー をご存知ですか。 *ii resutoran/baa o gozonji desu ka*
Is there a traditional Japanese/ inexpensive restaurant nearby?	この近くに料亭/安いレストランはありますか。 *kono chikaku ni ryootei/yasui resutoran wa arimasu ka*
A table for one/two, please.	一人/二人ですが、テーブルがありますか。 *hitori/futari desu ga, teeburu ga arimasu ka*
Could we sit...?	…に座れますか。 *...ni suwaremasu ka*
here/there	ここ/そこ *koko/soko*
outside	外 *soto*

in a non-smoking area	禁煙席
	kin en seki
I'm waiting for someone.	人を待っているんです。
	hito o matte irun desu
Where's the restroom [toilet]?	トイレはどこですか。
	toire wa doko desu ka
A menu, please.	メニューをお願いします。
	menyuu o onegai shimasu
What do you recommend?	何がおいしいですか。
	nani ga oishii desu ka
I'd like…	…が欲しいんですが
	…ga hoshiin desu ga
Some more…, please.	…をお願いします。
	…o onegai shimasu
Enjoy your meal.	どうぞごゆっくり。
	doozo goyukkuri
The check [bill], please.	お勘定、お願いします。
	okanjoo onegai shimasu
Is service included?	サービス料込みですか。
	saabisuryoo komi desu ka
Can I pay by credit card?	クレジットカードを使えますか。
	kurejitto kaado o tsukaemasu ka
Could I have a receipt, please?	レシートをお願いします。
	reshiito o onegai shimasu
Thank you for the food.	ごちそうさまでした。
	gochisoo sama deshita

WHERE TO EAT

Can you recommend…?	…はありますか。
	…wa arimasu ka

a restaurant	レストラン
	resutoran
a bar	バー
	baa
a cafe	カフェ
	kafe
a fast-food place	ファストフードの店
	fasuto fuudo no mise
a sushi restaurant	寿司屋
	sushi ya
a cheap restaurant	安いレストラン
	yasui resutoran
an expensive restaurant	高いレストラン
	takai resutoran
a restaurant with a good view	眺めの良いレストラン
	nagame no yoi resutoran
an authentic/ a non-touristy restaurant	庶民的な/観光客向けでないレストラン
	syominteki na/kankookyaku muke de nai resutoran

RESERVATIONS & PREFERENCES

I'd like to reserve a table...	…予約をお願いしたいんですが。
	yoyaku o onegai shitai n desu ga
for 2	2人で
	futari de
for this evening	今晩
	konban
for tomorrow at...	明日…時に
	ashita…ji ni
Can I get a table in the shade/sun?	日陰の/日向のテーブルをお願いします。
	hikage no/hinata no teeburu o onegai shimasu

YOU MAY HEAR...

ご予約はいただいておりますでしょうか。 Do you have a
goyoyaku wa itadaite orimasu deshoo ka reservation?
何人様でしょうか。 How many?
nannin sama deshoo ka
喫煙席と禁煙席のどちらがよろしいですか。 Smoking or
kitsuenseki to kin-enseki no dochira ga non-smoking?
yoroshii desu ka
ご注文はお決まりですか。 Are you ready
gochuumon wa okimari desu ka to order?
何がよろしいですか。 What would
nani ga yoroshii desu ka you like?
…がお薦めです。 I recommend…
...ga osusume desu
どうぞごゆっくり。 Enjoy your
doozo goyukkuri meal.

A table for 2.	2人、お願いします。
	futari onegai shimasu
We have a reservation.	予約してあります。
	yoyaku shite arimasu
My name is…	…です。
	...desu
Could we sit…?	…に座れますか。
	...ni suwaremasu ka
here/there	ここ/そこ
	koko/soko
outside	外
	soto
in a non-smoking area	禁煙席
	kin enseki

by the window	窓際
	madogiwa
in the shade	日陰に
	hikage ni
in the sun	日向に
	hinata ni
Where are the restrooms [toilets]?	トイレはどこですか。
	toire wa doko desu ka

HOW TO ORDER

Waiter!/Waitress!	ちょっとすみません。
	chotto sumimasen
We're ready to order.	注文したいんですが。
	chuumon shitain desu ga
May I see the wine list, please?	ワインリストをお願いします。
	wain risuto o onegai shimasu
I'd like…	…が欲しいんですが 。
	…ga hoshiin desu ga
a bottle of…	…を一 本
	…o ippon
a carafe of…	…を一カラフ
	…o hito karafu
a glass of…	…一杯
	…ippai
The menu, please.	メニューをお願いします。
	menyuu o onegaishimasu
Do you have…?	…は、ありますか。
	…wa arimasu ka
a menu in English	英語のメニュー
	eigo no menyuu
a fixed price menu	セットメニュー
	setto menyuu

YOU MAY SEE...

カバーチャージ	cover charge
セット値段	fixed-price
メニュー	menu
本日のメニュー	menu of the day
サービス料金込(別)	service (not) included
スペシャル	specials

a children's menu	子供用のメニュー	
	kodomo yoo no menyuu	
What do you recommend?	何がおいしいですか。	
	nani ga oishii desu ka	
What's this?	これは何ですか。	
	kore wan nan desu ka	
What's in it?	何が入っていますか。	
	nani ga haitte imasu ka	
Is it spicy?	これは辛いですか。	
	kore wa karai desu ka	
Some more ..., please	…を、もう少しお願いします。	
	...o moo sukoshi onegai shimasu	
It's to go [take away].	持ち帰りです。	
	mochi kaeri desu	
With/Without...	…と/…無しで	
	...to/...nashi de	
I can't have...	…は食べられません。	
	...wa taberaremasen	
I'd like...	…が欲しいんですが。	
	...ga hoshiin desu ga	
More... please	…をもっとください。	
	...o motto kudasai	

For Drinks, see page 186.

COOKING METHODS

baked	焼き *yaki*
boiled	茹で *yude*
braised	蒸し煮 *mushini*
breaded	パン粉 *panko*
creamed	クリームソース *kuriimu soosu*
diced	さいの目切りの *sai no me giri no*
filleted	切り身の *kiri mi no*
fried	揚げ *age*
grilled	焼き *yaki*
poached	ポシェ *poshe*
roasted	ロースト *roosuto*
sautéed	炒めた *itameta*
smoked	薫製 *kunsei*
steamed	蒸し *mushi*
stewed	煮込み *nikomi*
stuffed	詰め物 *tsumemono*

DIETARY REQUIREMENTS

I am...	私は…です。
	watashi wa... desu
diabetic	糖尿病
	toonyoobyoo
lactose intolerant	乳糖不対症
	nyuutoo futaishoo
vegetarian	ベジタリアン
	bejitarian
vegan	ヴィーガン
	biigan
I'm allergic to...	…にアレルギーがあります。
	...ni arerugii ga arimasu
I can't eat...	…は食べられません。
	...wa taberaremasen
dairy	乳製品
	nyuuseehin
gluten	グルテン
	guruten
nuts	ナッツ
	nattsu
pork	豚肉
	buta niku
shellfish	貝類
	kairui
spicy foods	辛い食べ物
	karai tabemono
wheat	小麦
	komugi
Is it halal/kosher?	これはハラール/コーシャですか。
	kore wa haraaru/koosha desu ka
Do you have...?	…はありますか。
	...wa arimasu ka

skimmed milk	無脂肪乳
	mushiboo nyuu
whole milk	普通の牛乳
	futsuu no gyuunyuu
soya milk	豆乳
	toonyuu
I'm lactose intolerant…	私は乳製品アレルギーがあります。
	watashi ha nyuseihin arerugi ga arimasu.

DINING WITH CHILDREN

Do you have children's portions?	お子さまメニューはありますか 。
	okosama menyuu wa arimasu ka
A highchair, please.	子供のための椅子はありますか。
	kodomo no tame no isu wa arimasu ka
Where can I feed/ change the baby?	どこで授乳したら/おしめを取り替えたら いいでしょうか 。
	doko de junyuu shitara/oshime o torikaetara ii deshoo ka
Can you warm this?	これを暖めてください。
	kore o atatamete kudaasai

HOW TO COMPLAIN

How much longer will our food be?	後、どのくらいかかりますか。
	ato dono kurai kakarimasu ka
We can't wait any longer.	もう待てません。
	moo matemasen
We're leaving.	帰ります。
	kaerimasu
I didn't order this.	注文したのと違います。
	chuumon shitano to chigaimasu
I ordered…	…を注文しました。
	…o chuumon shimashita

I can't eat this.	これは、食べられません。
	kore wa taberaremasen
This is too...	…すぎます。
	...sugimasu
cold/hot	冷た/熱
	tsumeta/atsu
salty/spicy	塩辛/辛
	shio kara/kara
tough/bland	固/味が薄
	kata/aji ga usu
This isn't clean/ fresh.	きれい/新鮮じゃありません。
	kiree/shinsen ja arimasen

PAYING

The check [bill], please.	お勘定、お願いします。
	okanjoo onegai shimasu
We'd like to pay separately.	別々に、お願いします。
	betsubetsu ni onegai shimasu
It's all together.	一緒にお願いします。
	issho ni onegai shimasu
Is service included?	サービス料込みですか。
	saabisu ryoo komi desu ka
What's this amount for?	これは何の金額ですか。
	kore wa nan no kingaku desu ka
I didn't have that.	それは取りませんでした。
	sore wa torimasen deshita.
I had...	注文したのは…です。
	chuumon shita nowa...desu
Can I pay by credit card?	クレジットカードを使えますか。
	kurejitto kaado o tsukaemasu ka
Can I have an itemized bill/ a receipt?	明細書/レシートをお願いします。
	meesaisho/reshiito o onegai shimasu

That was a very good meal.	おいしかった。ごちそうさまでした。
	oishikatta. gochisoo sama deshita
I've already paid.	もう支払いは済ませました。
	moo shiharai wa sumase mashita

Tipping is not a Japanese custom, and there is no need to tip at most restaurants, bars and **izakaya** (taverns). However, some places, especially high-end ones, may include a 'service charge' on the bill as gratuity.

MEALS & COOKING

In large Western-style hotels you will have your choice of breakfast: Japanese, English/American or Continental. However, in **ryokan** and **minshuku** (traditional Japanese lodgings) you will be offered only a Japanese-style breakfast. This usually consists of grilled, smoked fish (e.g. salmon), rice, soup and pickles served with tea. While you are out and about, coffee shops provide various dishes for breakfast, including thick slices of buttered toast.

BREAKFAST

ベーコン	bacon
beekon	
パン	bread
pan	

バター	butter
bataa	
(コールド/ホット)シリアル	(cold/hot) cereal
(koorudo/hotto) shiriaru	
チーズ	cheese
chiizu	
コーヒー/紅茶	coffee/tea
koohii/koocha	
砂糖入りの	with sugar
satoo iri no	
ダイエットシュガー 入りの	with artificial
daietto shugaa iri no	sweetner
ミルク入りの	with milk
miruku iri no	
カフェイン抜きの	decaf
kafein nuki no	
ブラック	black
burakku	
コールドカット	cold cuts
koorudo katto	[charcuterie]
卵	eggs
tamago	
ゆで卵	a boiled egg
yude tamago	
目玉焼き/スクランブルエッグ	fried/scrambled
medama yaki/sukuranburu eggu	eggs
フルーツジュース	fruit juice
furuutsu juusu	
アップル	apple
appuru	
グレープフルーツ	grapefruit
gureepufuruutsu	
オレンジ	orange
orenji	

グラノーラ *guranoora*	granola [muesli]
蜂蜜 *hachimitsu*	honey
ジャム *jamu*	jam
ミルク *miruku*	milk
マフィン *mafin*	muffin
オートミール *ooto miiru*	oatmeal
オムレツ *omuretsu*	omelet
ロールパン *rooru pan*	rolls
ソーセージ *sooseeji*	sausages
トースト *toosuto*	toast
水 *mizu*	water
ヨーグルト *yooguruto*	yogurt

APPETIZERS

オードブルの盛り合わせ *oodoburu no moriawase*	assorted appetizers
ハム *hamu*	ham
…が欲しいんですが 。 *…ga hoshiin desu ga*	I'd like…

…をもっとください。 *...o motto kudasai*	More… please
おつまみ *otsumami*	Japanese snacks
漬物 *tsukemono*	Japanese pickled vegetables
オリーブ *oriibu*	olives
牡蛎 *kaki*	oysters
サラダ *sarada*	salad
サラミ *sarami*	salami

> ⓘ
>
> **Otsumami** are snacks that accompany drinks. You will find such things as salted rice crackers, nuts and dried cuttle fish.

SOUP

コンソメスープ *konsome suupu*	clear soup
ポタージュスープ *potaaju suupu*	creamed soup
すまし汁(お吸物) *sumashi jiru (osuimono)*	Japanese clear soup
みそ汁 *misoshiru*	miso soup
コーンスープ *koon suupu*	sweetcorn soup

(i)

There are two kinds of Japanese soup, which is always part of a traditional meal: **misoshiru**, a light soup often with a few finely chopped pieces of vegetable and bean curd, the distinctive flavor of which comes from the fermented bean paste (**miso**); and **sumashi jiru** or **suimono**, a clear soup, again with vegetables or bean curd.

In a Japanese meal the soup is not served as a first course, but together with the main course, or with boiled rice and other items.

野菜スープ *yasai suupu*	vegetable soup
寄せ鍋 *yosenabe*	thick soup of chicken, shellfish, prawns, bean curd and vegetables
ラーメン *raamen*	Chinese noodle broth with meat, fish, veg
吸物/すまし汁 *suimono/sumashi jiru*	clear soup of fish bouillon or seaweed
あんかけうどん *ankake udon*	wheat noodles in a thick bouillon with fish cake and vegetables
タンメン *tanmen*	Chinese noodle soup with fried veg
冷麦 *hiyamugi*	thinly cut wheat noodles and cold soup

ざるそば *zaru soba*	buckwheat noodles served with cold soup
冷やし中華 *hiyashi chuuka*	Chinese noodles sweet and sour sauce, sliced ham, fish cake and cucumber
おでん *oden*	a winter soup with veg, fish cake, eggs

FISH & SEAFOOD

鰹(カツオ) *katsuo*	bonito (mackerel family)
鱈(タラ) *tara*	cod
たらこ *tarako*	cod roe
ロブスター *robusutaa*	lobster
鯖(サバ) *saba*	mackerel
ムール貝 *muuru gai*	mussels
蛸(タコ) *tako*	octopus
牡蠣(カキ) *kaki*	oysters
鮭(サケ) *sake*	salmon
いくら *ikura*	salmon roe
帆立貝 *hotate gai*	scallop

ⓘ

Fish and seafood play a major role in Japanese cuisine. This is reflected in the variety and quality of available seafood. Typical ways of eating fish include broiled, boiled, deep fried and raw. Prepared raw fish (**sushi** or **sashimi**) is dipped into a mixture of soy sauce and **wasabi** (horseradish paste), and enjoyed with steaming hot rice. **Sashimi** is usually served as part of a larger meal, and **sashimi** restaurants are often expensive. You can also buy **sushi** at the food court of a department store, at a supermarket, or at a take-out restaurant.

いか *ika*	squid
海老(エビ) *ebi*	shrimp [prawns]
鱒(マス) *masu*	trout
鮪(マグロ) *maguro*	tuna
白子(シラス) *shirasu*	whitebait
刺身 *sashimi*	raw fish with soy and wasabi
寿司 *sushi*	rice balls with raw fish
焼き魚 *yaki zakana*	grilled fish
天ぷら *tenpura*	fresh fish, seafood and veg, deep-fried
天ぷらうどん *tenpura udon*	battered fish and veg in a noodle broth

煮魚 *ni zakana*	fish cooked in assorted sauces
ちり鍋 *chirinabe*	fish and veg broth

MEAT & POULTRY

ベーコン *beekon*	bacon
牛肉 *gyuu niku*	beef
鶏肉/チキン *tori niku/chikin*	chicken
鴨 *kamo*	duck
ひれステーキ *hire suteeki*	filet steak
ハム *hamu*	ham
ラム肉 *ramu niku*	lamb
レバー *rebaa*	liver
豚肉 *buta niku*	pork
ソーセージ *sooseeji*	sausages
ステーキ *suteeki*	steak
サーロインステーキ *saaroin suteeki*	sirloin steak
薄切り *usugiri*	thin slices

すき焼 *sukiyaki*	thin slices of beef, veg, bean curd, noodles
しゃぶしゃぶ *shabu shabu*	thinly sliced beef with veg in broth
焼肉 *yaki niku*	Grilled Korean marinated meat, veg
とんかつ *tonkatsu*	fried breaded pork cutlet with cabbage and rice
カツ丼 *katsudon*	deep fried pork with rice, egg, onion,peas
焼き鳥 *yakitori*	barbequed chicken in sweet soy sauce
レア *rea*	rare
ミディアム *midiamu*	medium
ウェルダン *werudan*	well-done

VEGETABLES & STAPLES

おひたし *ohitashi*	boiled green vegetables with soy sauce
豆 *mame*	beans
パン *pan*	bread
そば *soba*	buckwheat noodles

(i)

In a Japanese meal, rice is served separately in an individual bowl. It is short grained and slightly sticky. Although plain, rice is perhaps the most important part of the meal. The Japanese consider it a heresy to mix other food items or sauces into the rice. It is customary to raise the bowl to your lips and push the rice into your mouth with chopsticks. On a Western-style menu rice is usually called **raisu**. For egg and rice dishes, see On the Menu on page 195 under 'egg'.

キャベツ	cabbage
kyabetsu	
にんじん	carrot
ninjin	
白菜	Chinese cabbage
hakusai	
ラーメン	Chinese noodles in soup
raamen	
きゅうり	cucumber
kyuuri	
なす	eggplant [aubergine]
nasu	
ぎんなん	gingko nut
ginnan	
さやいんげん	green bean
saya ingen	
漬物	Japanese pickled vegetables
tsukemono	
ねぎ	leek
negi	
レタス	lettuce
retasu	

Salad isn't part of traditional Japanese cuisine;
pickled vegetables are a more authentic equivalent.
However, many Western-style restaurants and bars offer a
variety of salads and dressings.

パスタ *pasuta*	pasta
味の素 *aji no moto*	MSG (monosodium glutamate)
マッシュルーム *masshuruumu*	mushroom
椎茸(しいたけ) *shiitake*	shitake mushroom
えのきだけ *enokidake*	enokidake mushroom
玉ねぎ *tamanegi*	onion
グリンピース *gurinpiisu*	pea
ポテト *poteto*	potato (in Western dishes)
じゃがいも *jagaimo*	potato (in Japanese dishes)
かぼちゃ *kabocha*	pumpkin
ご飯 *gohan*	rice
スパゲッティ *supagetti*	spaghetti
野菜炒め *yasai itame*	stir-fried vegetables

野菜の煮物 *yasai no nimono*	stewed vegetables
トマト *tomato*	tomato
大根 *daikon*	white radish
うどん *udon*	wheat noodles

Noodle dishes are very popular, and make delicious and filling meals. It's not considered bad manners to make slurping noises while eating your noodles — the extra oxygen is supposed to improve the taste. For dishes, see 'noodle' on page 200 in the On the Menu section.

FRUIT

りんご *ringo*	apple
バナナ *banana*	banana
さくらんぼ *sakuranbo*	cherry
グレープフルーツ *gureepufuruutsu*	grapefruit
ぶどう *budoo*	grape
メロン *meron*	melon
オレンジ *orenji*	orange

桃 *momo*	peach
梨 *nashi*	pear
柿 *kaki*	persimmon
苺(いちご) *ichigo*	strawberry
蜜柑(みかん) *mikan*	tangerine
西瓜(すいか) *suika*	watermelon

DESSERT

餅 *mochi*	rice cake, traditionally eaten at New Year
あんみつ *anmitsu*	gelatin cubes made from seaweed, with sweet bean paste and fruit
氷あずき *koori azuki*	sweet bean paste covered with shaved ice and sweet syrup
フルーツみつ豆 *furuutsu mitsumame*	gelatin cubes made from seaweed, topped with fruit and syrup
プリン *purin*	crème caramel
アイスクリーム *aisu kuriimu*	ice cream

ⓘ

Dessert is not a typical part of a Japanese meal.
Called **dezaato**, it was introduced from the West. Today
you will find a variety of Western-style desserts along with
a number of desserts made from more typical Japanese
ingredients.

あんまん *anman*	hot steamed bun with sweet azuki bean paste
チョコレートパフェ *chokoreeto pafe*	chocolate parfait
葛餅 *kuzu moch*	arrowroot cake with molasses syrup
ホットケーキ *hotto keeki*	sweet pancake with butter and syrup
フルーツサラダ *furuutsu sarada*	fruit salad
おはぎ *ohagi*	balls of rice covered with bean paste
お汁粉 *oshiruko*	sweet red bean paste soup

SAUCES & CONDIMENTS

コショウ/胡椒 *koshoo*	black pepper
ケチャップ *kechappu*	ketchup
味噌 *miso*	miso (paste of fermented soybeans)

マスタード　　　　　　　　　　mustard
masutaado
塩　　　　　　　　　　　　　　salt
shio
醤油　　　　　　　　　　　　　soy sauce
shooyu

ⓘ

In Japan, goods are usually sold in small portions to avoid selling them in certain numbers as some numbers are considered bad luck. Vegetables are usually sold per piece, or in pre-packaged bags that are quite uniform in volume. The weight is not marked (e.g. a bag of potatoes contains five potatoes). Prices for fish vary according to type and season and are sold per unit, not by the kilogram.

AT THE MARKET

Where are the carts [trolleys]/baskets?	カート/かごはどこですか。 *kaato/kago wa doko desu ka*
Where is…?	…はどこですか。 *…wa doko desu ka*
I'd like some of that/those.	それを少しください。 *sore o sukoshi kudasai*
Can I taste it?	味見してもいいですか。 *ajimi shitemo ii desu ka*
I'd like a kilo/half-kilo of …	…が一キロ/五百グラム欲しいんですが *…ga ichikiro/gohyakuguramu hoshiin desu ga*
I'd like…	…が欲しいんですが *…ga hoshiin desu ga*
a liter/half-liter of…	…が一リットル/500cc *… ga iti rittoru/gohyaku shiishii*

a piece of	…が一個
	…ga ikko
a slice of	…が一枚
	…ga ichimai
More/Less than that	もう少し多く/少なく
	moo sukoshi ooku/sukunaku
How much?	いくらですか。
	ikura desuka
Where do I pay?	どこで払うんですか。
	doko de haraun desu ka
A bag, please.	袋をお願いします。
	fukuro o onegai shimasu
I'm being helped.	大丈夫です。
	daijoobu desu

YOU MAY SEE…

賞味期限…	best if used by…
カロリー	calories
無脂肪	fat free
要冷蔵	keep refrigerated
…を極少量含む	may contain traces of…
販売期限	sell by…
菜食主義者向け	suitable for vegetarians

YOU MAY HEAR...

いらっしゃいませ。   Can I help you?
irasshaimase
何がよろしいですか。   What would
naniga yoroshii desu ka   you like?
他に何かございますか。   Anything else?
hokani nanika gozaimasu ka
…円でございます。   That's…yen.
…en de gozaimasu

For daily shopping, people usually go to a
neighborhood fish market, vegetable store, butcher or
grocer. Larger supermarkets are also popular, as well
as food floors of department stores (usually located in
the basement) where you'll find groceries and prepared
food. In Tokyo there is a famous fish market called **Tsukiji
Uoichiba**, which is open early in the morning. In Kyoto,
Nishiki Shijo (Nishiki Market) is called the kitchen of
Kyoto. Here you can find all kinds of local ingredients at
more than one hundred stores.

IN THE KITCHEN

bottle opener	栓抜き
	sennuki
bowl	ボール
	booru
can opener	缶切り
	kankiri
corkscrew	コルクスクリュー
	koruku sukuryuu
cups	カップ
	kappu
forks	フォーク
	fooku
frying pan	フライパン
	furaipan
glasses	グラス/コップ
	gurasu/koppu
knife	ナイフ
	naifu
measuring cup/ spoon	計量カップ/スプーン
	keeryoo kappu/supuun
napkin	ナプキン
	napukin
plates	皿
	sara
pot	深鍋
	fuka nabe
saucepan	鍋
	nabe
spatula	へら
	hera
spoon	スプーン
	supuun

DRINKS

NEED TO KNOW

May I see the wine list/drink menu?	ワインリスト/ドリンクメニュー を見せて ください。 *wain risuto/dorinku menyuu o misete kudasai*
What do you recommend?	何がおいしいですか。 *nani ga oishii desu ka*
I'd like a bottle/glass of red/white wine.	赤/白ワインを一本/一杯お願いします。 *aka/shiro wain o ippon/ippai onegai shimasu*
The house wine, please.	ハウスワインをお願いします。 *hausu wain o onegai shimasu*
Another bottle/glass, please.	もう一本/一杯お願いします。 *moo ippon/ippai onegai shimasu*
I'd like a local beer.	地ビールをお願いします。 *jibiiru o onegai shimasu*
Can I buy you a drink?	一杯おごらせてください。 *ippai ogorasete kudasai*
Cheers!	乾杯! *kanpai*
A coffee/tea, please.	コーヒー/紅茶をお願いします。 *koohii/koocha o onegai shimasu*
Black	ブラック *burakku*
With…	…と *…to*
milk	ミルク *miruku*
sugar	砂糖 *satoo*

artificial sweetener	ダイエットシュガー
	daietto shugaa
With/Without...	…と/…無しで
	...to/...nashi de
I can't have...	…は食べられません
	...wa taberaremasen
I'd like...	…をお願いします。
	...o onegai shimasu
juice	フルーツジュース
	furuutsu juusu
soda	炭酸飲料
	tansan inryoo
sparkling/still water	ソーダ水/水
	soda sui/mizu
Is the tap water safe to drink?	水道水は飲んでも安全ですか。
	suidoosui wa nondemo anzen desu ka

NON-ALCOHOLIC DRINKS

コーヒー	coffee
koohii	
ブラック	black
burakku	
ミルク入りの	with milk
miruku irino	
砂糖入りの	with sugar
satoo iri no	
ダイエットシュガー入りの	with artificial
daietto shugaa iri no	sweetner
アイスコーヒー	iced coffee
aisu koohii	

(i)

Sake is the general name for any drink, traditional or imported, but is usually used to refer to rice wine, more properly known as **nihonshu**.

Japanese green tea is often served in restaurants free of charge. It is drunk without any additions.

A special tea, **matcha** is used for traditional ceremonies. It was first used by Buddhist monks to help them stay awake while meditating. Its spiritual roots are still apparent today in the highly ritualized tea ceremony. The tea should not only refresh you physically, but also give you time to appreciate the beauty of the objects used in the ceremony and the surroundings, all leading to meditative reflection. You may find tea ceremony rooms in museums and gardens, where you'll be able to try a little **matcha** for a small fee.

ココア *kokoa*	hot chocolate
ジュース *juusu*	juice
アップルジュース *appuru juusu*	apple juice
オレンジジュース *orenji juusu*	orange juice
レモネード *remoneedo*	lemonade
ミルク *miruku*	milk (when ordering at a restaurant)
ミルクセーキ *mirukuseeki*	milkshake
紅茶 *koocha*	tea

お茶 *ocha*	green tea
アイスティー *aisu tii*	iced tea
水 *mizu*	water
ミネラルウォーター *mineraru wootaa*	mineral water
ソーダ *sooda*	soda water
トニック *tonikku*	tonic water

YOU MAY HEAR...

何か飲みますか。 *nani ka nomimasu ka*	Can I get you a drink?
ミルク/砂糖を入れますか。 *miruku/satoo o iremasu ka*	With milk/sugar?
炭酸水ですか,非炭酸水ですか。 *tansansui desu ka hi tansansui desu ka*	Sparkling or still water?

APERITIFS, COCKTAILS & LIQUEURS

シングル/ダブル *shinguru/daburu*	single/double
ストレート/オンザロック *sutoreeto/onzarokku*	straight [neat]/on the rocks
グラス1杯/瓶1本 *gurasu ippai/bin ippon*	a glass/a bottle
ブランデー *burandee*	brandy

ジン *jin*	gin
ジントニック *jin tonikku*	gin and tonic
梅酒 *umeshu*	plum wine
ラム酒 *ramu shu*	rum
シェリー/ベルモット *sherii/berumotto*	sherry/vermouth
焼酎 *shoochuu*	shoochuu
ウォッカ *wokka*	vodka
ウイスキー *uisukii*	whisky
水割り *mizuwari*	with water
ウイスキーソーダ *uisukii sooda*	with soda water

BEER

瓶入り *bin iri*	bottled
生 *nama*	draft [draught]
黒ビール *kuro biiru*	dark beer

WINE

赤ワイン *aka wain*	red wine

(i)

The Japanese produce a number of different beers which are similar to English and German lager beers. Three well known-brands are Asahi®, Kirin® and Sapporo®. In most bars you can choose between bottled and draft. **Shoochuu** is a distilled liquor (up to 90 proof) made from either sweet potatoes or rice. This drink is not commonly known to visitors to Japan and is held in rather low esteem by some Japanese. The best **shoochuu** is, however, excellent and is comparable to tequila, vodka, and other such spirits. Whisky is now a very popular drink in Japan and there are a number of good Japanese brands — the best known is probably Suntory®.

(i)

Grape wine isn't an authentic Japanese drink and until recently was not produced in Japan. You will not find wine widely available outside of Western-style restaurants, big hotels, and department stores. Even there you may find the choice limited to sweeter white wines, although this is changing.

Rice wine, known as **nihonshu** but usually referred to as **sake**, is the traditional Japanese wine. The snacks traditionally served with sake are known as **otsumami**. These include seafood and meat served on skewers, sweet-salty dried cuttlefish, sashimi and more.

This drink is served at table in small china carafes and is drunk from small cups or wooden boxes. You can ask for your **nihonshu** to be served cold, warm or hot.

白ワイン *shiro wain*	white wine
ロゼ *roze*	blush [rosé] wine
ドライ/スイート/スパークリング *dorai/suiito/supaakuringu*	dry/sweet/ sparkling
冷えた/室温の *hieta/shitsuon no*	chilled/at room temperature
お酒/日本酒 *osake/nihonshu*	sake/nihonshu
冷 *hiya*	cold
人肌 *hitohada*	lukewarm
熱燗 *atsukan*	hot

ON THE MENU

アーモンド *aamondo*	almond
食前酒 *shokuzenshu*	aperitif
りんご *ringo*	apple
アップルジュース *appuru juusu*	apple juice
アンズ *anzu*	apricot
アーティチョーク *aatichooku*	artichoke
ダイエットシュガー *daietto shugaa*	artificial sweetner

アスパラバス *asuparagasu*	asparagus
アボカド *abokado*	avocado
ベーコン *beekon*	bacon
バナナ *banana*	banana
バス *basu*	bass
ベイリーフ *bei riifu*	bay leaf
豆 *mame*	bean
もやし *moyashi*	bean sprout
牛肉 *gyuu niku*	beef
ビール *biiru*	beer
ビート *biito*	beet
胡椒 *koshoo*	black pepper
ロゼ *roze*	blush [rosé] wine
鰹(カツオ) *katsuo*	bonito (mackerel family)
ブランデー *burandee*	brandy
パン *pan*	bread
胸肉 *muneniku*	breast chicken

コンソメ	broth
konsome	
そば	buckwheat noodles
soba	
バター	butter
bataa	
キャベツ	cabbage
kyabetsu	
にんじん	carrot
ninjin	
カリフラワー	cauliflower
karifurawaa	
セロリ	celery
serori	
チーズ	cheese
chiizu	
さくらんぼ	cherry
sakuranbo	
鶏肉	chicken
tori niku	
ひよこ豆	chickpea
hiyoko mame	
白菜	Chinese cabbage
hakusai	
餃子	Chinese meat dumplings
gyooza	
ラーメン	Chinese noodle soup
raamen	
チョコレート	chocolate
chokoreeto	
鱈(タラ)	cod
tara	
たらこ	cod roe
tarako	

コーヒー *koohii*	coffee
クッキー *kukkii*	cookie [biscuit]
コーンミール *koon miiru*	cornmeal
蟹 *kani*	crab
クラッカー *kurakkaa*	cracker
生クリーム *namakuriimu*	cream
きゅうり *kyuuri*	cucumber
カレー *karee*	curried
カスタード *kasutaado*	custard
揚げ *age*	deep-fried
するめ *surume*	dried squid
鴨 *kamo*	duck
餃子 *gyooza*	dumpling
鰻 *unagi*	eel
卵 *tamago*	egg
卵焼き *tamago yaki*	thick sweet omelet
目玉焼き *medama yaki*	fried eggs

オムレツ *omuretsu*	omelet
オムライス *omuraisu*	omelet with fried fried rice and ketchup
茶碗蒸し *chawan mushi*	egg custard with veg, fish and chicken
定食 *teeshoku*	set menu: rice, soup, fish or meat, pickles
炒飯 *chaahan*	fried rice with pork, egg, peas and shrimp
カレーライス *karee raisu*	Japanese curry
なす *nasu*	eggplant [aubergine]
エンダイブ *endaibu*	endive
キクヂシャ *kikujisha*	escarole
いちじく *ichijiku*	fig
魚 *sakana*	fish
蒲鉾 *kamaboko*	fish cake
ポテトフライ *poteto furai*	French fries [chips]
フルーツ/果物 *furuutsu/kudamono*	fruit
フルーツサラダ *furuutsu sarada*	fruit salad

ニンニク *ninniku*	garlic
ジン *jin*	gin
生姜 *shooga*	ginger
ぎんなん *ginnan*	gingko nuts
グラノーラ *guranoora*	granola [muesli]
グレープフルーツ *gureepufuruutsu*	grapefruit
ぶどう/葡萄 *budoo*	grape
さやいんげん *saya ingen*	green bean
お茶 *ocha*	green tea
焼き豆腐 *yaki doofu*	grilled tofu
グアバ *guaba*	guava
ハム *hamu*	ham
ハンバーガー *hanbaagaa*	hamburger
ヘーゼルナッツ *heezeru nattsu*	hazlenut
心臓 *shinzoo*	heart
ハーブ *haabu*	herb
ニシン *nishin*	herring

蜂蜜(ハニー)	honey
hachimitsu (hanii)	
ココア	hot chocolate
kokoa	
ホットドッグ	hot dog
hotto doggu	
氷	ice (cube)
koori	
アイスクリーム	ice cream
aisu kuriimu	
アイスコーヒー	iced coffee
aisu koohii	
アイスティー	iced tea
aisu tii	
ジャム	jam
jamu	
漬物	Japanese pickled
tsukemono	
vegetables	
おつまみ	Japanese snacks
otsumami	
カレーライス	Japanese-style
karee raisu	
curry on rice	
ジュース	juice
juusu	
ケチャップ	ketchup
kechappu	
キウィ	kiwi
kiui	
ラム肉	lamb
ramu niku	
ねぎ/葱	leek
negi	

もも肉 *momo niku*	leg
レモン *remon*	lemon
レモネード *remoneedo*	lemonade
平豆 *hiramame*	lentil
レタス *retasu*	lettuce
ライム *raimu*	lime
レバー *rebaa*	liver
ロブスター *robusutaa*	lobster
鯖(サバ) *saba*	mackerel
マンゴー *mangoo*	mango
マーガリン *maagarin*	margerine
マヨネーズ *mayoneezu*	mayonnaise
肉 *niku*	meat
メロン *meron*	melon
牛乳 *gyuunyuu*	milk (a carton)
ミルク *miruku*	milk (when ordering in a restaurant)
ミルクセーキ *mirukuseeki*	milkshake

ミネラルウォーター *mineraru wootaa*	mineral water
ミント *minto*	mint
味噌 *miso*	miso (paste made from fermented soybeans)
みそ汁 *misoshiru*	miso soup
味の素 *aji no moto*	MSG (monosodium glutamate)
マッシュルーム *masshuruumu*	mushrooms
ムール貝 *muuru gai*	mussels
からし *karashi*	mustard
マトン *maton*	mutton
うどん *udon*	noodle
そば *soba*	buckwheat noodle broth, meat or egg, veg
うどん *udon*	wheat-flour noodle broth, meat or egg, veg
ラーメン *raamen*	Chinese noodle broth
そうめん *soomen*	wheat-flour noodles
ヌガー *nugaa*	nougat

ナッツ	nuts
nattsu	
オートミール	oatmeal
ootomiiru	
蛸(タコ)	octopus
tako	
オリーブ	olive
oriibu	
オリーブオイル	olive oil
oriibu oiru	
オムレツ	omelet
omuretsu	
玉ねぎ	onion
tamanegi	
オレンジ	orange
orenji	
オレンジジュース	orange juice
orenji juusu	
オレガノ	oregano
oregano	
オックス	ox
okkusu	
オックステール	oxtail
okkusu teeru	
牡蛎	oyster
kaki	
パンケーキ	pancake
pankeeki	
パパイヤ	papaya
papaiya	
パプリカ	paprika
papurika	
パスタ	pasta
pasuta	

ペストリー *pesutorii*	pastry
桃 *momo*	peach
ピーナッツ *piinattsu*	peanut
梨 *nashi*	pear (Japanese pears)
グリンピース *gurinpiisu*	pea
ピーカン *piikan*	pecan
ピーマン *pepper*	pepper (vegetable)
柿 *kaki*	persimmon
ピクルス *pikurusu*	pickle [gherkin]
パイナップル *painappuru*	pineapple
ピザ *piza*	pizza
プラム *puramu*	plum
豚肉 *buta niku*	pork
馬鈴薯/じゃがいも *bareesho/jagaimo*	potato (Japanese dishes)
ポテト *poteto*	potato (Western dishes)
ポテトチップ *poteto chippu*	potato chips [crisps]
プルーン *puruun*	prune

プリン *purin*	pudding
かぼちゃ *kabocha*	pumpkin
ウズラ *uzura*	quail
ウサギ肉 *usagi niku*	rabbit
ラディッシュ *radisshu*	radish
レーズン *reezun*	raisin
レリッシュ *rerisshu*	relish
ご飯 *gohan*	rice
煎餅 *senbee*	rice crackers
ロースト *roosuto*	roast
ローストビーフ *roosuto biifu*	roast beef
ロールパン *rooru pan*	roll
ラム酒 *ramu shu*	rum
サラダ *sarada*	salad
サラミ *sarami*	salami
鮭(サケ) *sake*	salmon
いくら *ikura*	salmon roe

塩 *shio*	salt
サンドイッチ *sandoitchi*	sandwich
イワシ *iwashi*	sardine
ソース *soosu*	sauce
ソーセージ *sooseeji*	sausage
お好み焼き *okonomiyaki*	savory pancakes
ねぎ *negi*	scallion [spring onion]
帆立貝 *hotate gai*	scallop
スコッチ *sukotchi*	scotch
魚介類/海鮮料理 *gyokai rui/kaisen ryoori*	seafood
海苔 *nori*	seaweed (dried)
シェリー *sherii*	sherry
椎茸(しいたけ) *shiitake*	shitake mushroom
海老 *ebi*	shrimp [prawns]
炭酸飲料 *tansan inryoo*	soda
ソーダ *sooda*	soda water
スープ *suupu*	soup

醤油 *shooyu*	soy (sauce)
スパゲッティ *supagetti*	spaghetti
ほうれん草 *hoorensoo*	spinach
かぼちゃ *kabocha*	squash
いか *ika*	squid
ステーキ *suteeki*	steak
苺(いちご) *ichigo*	strawberry
砂糖 *satoo*	sugar
甘いもの *amaimono*	sweets
サツマイモ *satsumaimo*	sweet potato
メカジキ *mekajiki*	swordfish
シロップ *shiroppu*	syrup
蜜柑(みかん) *mikan*	tangerine
タラゴン *taragon*	tarragon
紅茶 *koocha*	tea (black)
トースト *toosuto*	toast
タイム *taimu*	thyme

豆腐 *toofu*	tofu (soybean curd)
トマト *tomato*	tomato
トニック *tonikku*	tonic water
胃袋 *ibukuro*	tripe
鱒(マス) *masu*	trout
トリュフ *toryufu*	truffles
鮪(マグロ) *maguro*	tuna
七面鳥 *shichimenchoo*	turkey
かぶ *kabu*	turnip
バニラ *banira*	vanilla
子牛の肉 *koushinoniku*	veal
野菜 *yasai*	vegetable
鹿の肉 *shika no niku*	venison
ベルモット *berumotto*	vermouth
ウォッカ *wokka*	vodka
酢 *su*	vinegar
水 *mizu*	water

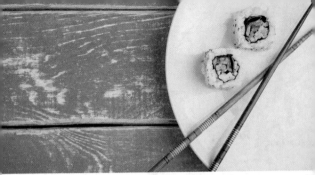

クレソン	watercress
kureson	
西瓜(すいか)	watermelon
suika	
小麦	wheat
komugi	
うどん	wheat noodles
udon	
ウイスキー	whisky
uisukii	
大根	white radish
daikon	
白子(シラス)	whitebait
shirasu	
猪	wild boar
inoshishi	
ワイン	wine
wain	
ヨーグルト	yogurt
yooguruto	
ズッキーニ	zucchini [courgette]
zukkiini	

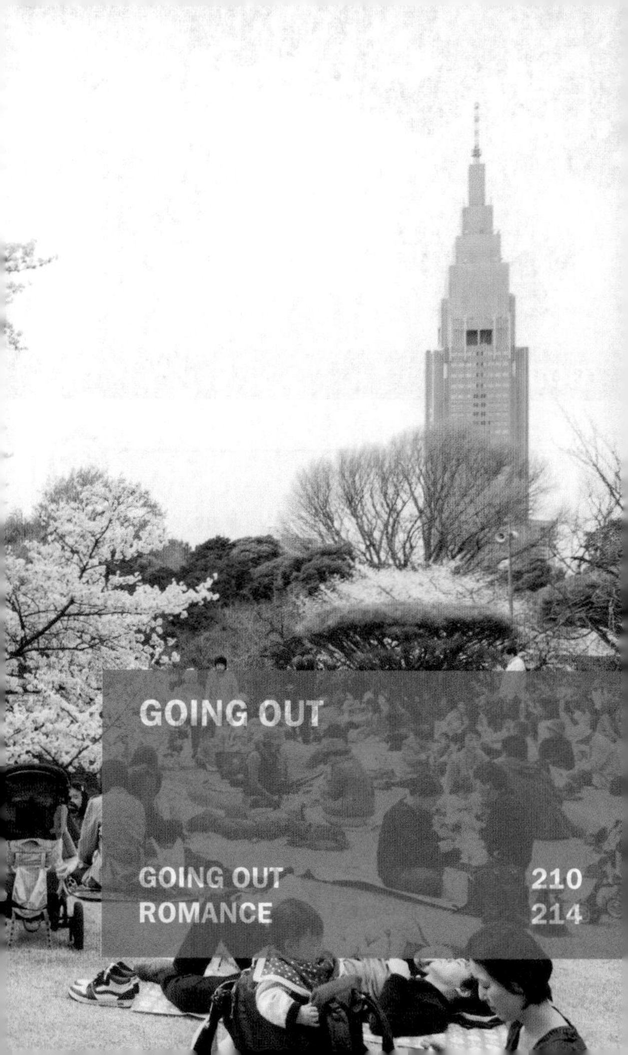

GOING OUT

GOING OUT

NEED TO KNOW

What is there to do in the evenings?	夜は 何がありますか。 *yoru wa nani ga arimasu ka*
Do you have a program of events?	催し物のプログラムがありますか。 *moyooshimono no puroguramu gaarimasu ka*
What's playing at the movies [cinema] tonight?	今晩、どんな映画をやっていますか。 *konban donna eega o yatte imasu ka*
Where's...?	…はどこですか。 *...wa doko desu ka*
the downtown area	繁華街 *hankagai*
the bar	バー *baa*
the dance club	ディスコ *disuko*
Is there a cover charge?	カバーチャージはありますか。 *kabaa chaaji wa arimasu ka*

ENTERTAINMENT

Can you recommend…?	…はありますか。
	…wa arimasu ka
a concert	コンサート
	konsaato
a movie	映画
	eega
an opera	オペラ
	opera
a play	芝居
	shibai
When does it start/ end?	いつ始まりますか/終わりますか。
	itsu hajimarimasu ka/owarimasu ka
What's the dress code?	服装規定がありますか。
	fukusoo kitei ga arimasu ka
I like …	…が好きです。
	…ga suki desu
classical music	クラシック音楽
	kurashikku ongaku
folk music	フォーク
	fooku
jazz	ジャズ
	jazu

If you are looking for popular music and dancing you'll find good quality jazz clubs and conventional discos, even country and- western bars, all in Tokyo's cosmopolitan restaurant districts of Akasaka and Roppongi. Teenagers might like to join in the open-air dancing at Harajuku, near Yoyogi Park.

ⓘ

There are many local and regional festivals throughout the year in Japan. Some examples are; the Snow Festival in Sapporo, from late February to mid-March. In late March to early April the famous Japanese cherry blossoms invite everyone out to enjoy. In May, Kyoto has the Aoi Festival, one of three festivals that reenact Kyoto's history. The other two are the Jidai Festival in October and Gion Festival in July.

pop music	ポピュラー音楽	
	popyuraa ongaku	
rap	ラップ音楽	
	rappu ongaku	

NIGHTLIFE

What is there to do in the evenings?	夜は何がありますか。	
	yoru wa nani ga arimasu ka	
Can you recommend…?	いい…はありますか。	
	ii…wa arimasu ka	
a bar	バー	
	baa	
a dance club	ディスコ	
	disuko	
a gay club	ゲイバー	
	gee baa	
a jazz club	ジャズクラブ	
	jazu kurabu	
a karaoke bar	カラオケバー	
	karaoke baa	
a club with Japanese music	日本の音楽が聴けるクラブ	
	nihon no ongaku ga kikeru kurabu	

Is there live music?	生演奏がありますか。
	nama ensoo ga arimasu ka
How do I get there?	どうやって行くんですか。
	dooyatte ikun desu ka
Is there a cover charge?	カバーチャージはありますか。
	kabaa chaaji wa arimasu ka
Let's go dancing.	ダンスをしに行きましょう。
	dansu o shini ikimashoo
Is this area safe at night?	このあたりは、夜、安全ですか。
	kono atari wa yoru anzen desu ka

YOU MAY HEAR...

携帯電話をお切りください。
keitaidenwa o okiri kudasai

Turn off your cell [mobile] phones, please.

Japan has a wide variety of traditional arts and culture. Some examples from nature are: **bonsai**, an art to recreate nature on a small scale using plants; Japanese gardens, peaceful natural scenes located in cities or temples and **ikebana** or flower arrangement. If you prefer performances, don't miss **bunraku**, puppet theater using dolls of about three feet tall, manipulated by people on the stage. And of course there is **kabuki**, traditional Japanese theater.

ROMANCE

NEED TO KNOW

Would you like to go out for a drink/meal?	飲み物/食事はいかがですか。 *nomimono/shokuji wa ikaga desu ka*
What are your plans for tonight/tomorrow?	今晩/明日予定はありますか。 *konban/ashita yotee wa arimasu ka*
Can I have your number?	電話番号を教えてくれませんか。 *denwa bangoo o oshiete kuremasen ka*
Can I join you?	ご一緒してもいいですか。 *goissho shitemo ii desu ka*
Can I buy you a drink?	一杯おごらせてください。 *ippai ogorasete kudasai*
I like you.	あなたが気に入りました。 *anata ga kini irimashita*
I love you.	あなたが好きです。 *anata ga suki desu*

THE DATING GAME

Would you like to...?	行きませんか。
	...ikimasen ka
go out for coffee	コーヒーを飲みに
	koohii o nomi ni
go for a drink	飲みに
	nomi ni
go out for a meal	食事に
	shokuji ni
What are your for...?	...予定はありますか。
	...yotee wa arimasu ka
today	今日
	kyoo
tonight	今晩
	konban
tomorrow	明日
	ashita
this weekend	今週末
	konshuumatsu
Where would you like to go?	どこに行きましょうか。
	doko ni ikimashoo ka
I'd like to go to...	...に行きたいです。
	...ni ikitai desu
Do you like...?	...は好きですか。
	...wa suki desu ka
Can I have your number/e-mail?	電話番号/Eメールアドレスを教えてくれませんか。
	denwabangoo/iimeeru adoresu o oshiete kuremasen ka
Can I join you?	ご一緒してもいいですか。
	goissho shitemo ii desu ka
You're very attractive.	あなたはとても魅力的ですね。
	anata wa totemo miryokuteki desu ne

| Let's go somewhere quieter. | もっと静かなところへ行きましょう。 |
| | *motto shizukana tokoro e ikimasshoo* |

For Communications, see page 84.

ACCEPTING & REJECTING

I'd love to.	喜んで
	yorokonde
Where should we meet?	どこで待ち合わせましょうか。
	doko de machiawasemashoo ka
I'll meet you at the bar/your hotel.	バー/ホテルで会いましょう。
	baa/hoteru de aimashoo
I'll come by at…	…に来ます。
	…ni kimasu
What's your address?	住所は？
	juusho wa
Thank you, but I'm busy.	申し訳ありませんが、約束があります。
	mooshiwake arimasen ga yakusoku ga arimasu
I'm not interested.	興味がありません。
	kyuoomi ga arimasen
Leave me alone.	構わないでください。
	kamawanaide kudasai

Stop bothering me!	邪魔するのはやめてください。
	jama suru nowa yamete kudasai

GETTING INTIMATE

Can I hug/kiss you?	抱き締めても/キスしてもいいですか。
	dakishimetemo/kisushitemo ii desu ka
Yes.	はい
	hai
No.	いいえ
	iie
Stop!	やめて!
	yamete

SEXUAL PREFERENCES

Are you gay?	あなたはゲイですか。
	anata wa gee desu ka
I'm…	私は…です。
	watashi wa …desu
heterosexual	ヘテロ
	hetero
homosexual	ホモ
	homo
bisexual	バイ
	bai
Do you like men/women?	男性/女性が好きですか。
	dansei/josei ga suki desu ka

For Grammar, see page 14.

DICTIONARY

ENGLISH–JAPANESE

A

a.m. 午前 gozen

abbey 修道院 shuudooin

access v (Internet) アクセスします akusesu shimasu

accident 事故 jiko

accommodation 宿泊設備 shukuhaku setsubi

account n 会計 kaikee

acupuncture 鍼 hari

adapter アダプタ adaputa

address 住所 juusho

after …の後 …no ato

afternoon 午後 gogo

aftershave アフターシェーブ afutaa sheebu

age 年齢 nenree

agency 代理店 dairiten

AIDS エイズ eezu

air conditioning エアコン eakon

air pump エアポンプ eaponpu

airline 航空会社 kookuu gaisha

airmail 航空便 kookuubin

airplane 飛行機 hikooki

airport 空港 kuukoo

aisle 通路 tsuuro

aisle seat 通路側の座席 tsuurogawa no zaseki

allergic アレルギー arerugii

allergic reaction アレルギー反応 arerugii hannoo

alone 一人の人 hitori no hito

alter v (clothing) 直します naoshi masu

alternate route 他の道 hoka no michi

aluminum foil アルミホイル arumi hoiru

amazing すごい sugoi

ambulance 救急車 kyuukyuusha

American アメリカの amerika no

amusement park 遊園地 yuuenchi

anemic 貧血の hinketsu no

anesthesia 麻酔 masui

animal 動物 doobutsu

ankle 足首 ashikubi

antibiotic 抗生物質 koosee busshitsu

antiques store 骨董店 kottooten

adj adjective	**BE** British English	**prep** preposition
adv adverb	**n** noun	**v** verb

antiseptic cream 傷薬 kizugusuri

anything 何でも nandemo

apartment マンション manshon

appendix (body part) 盲腸 moochoo

appetizer おつまみ otsumami

appointment 予約 yoyaku

arcade アーケード aakeedo

area code 市外局番 shigai kyokuban

arm 腕 ude

aromatherapy アロマセラピー aroma serapii

around (the corner) 道を曲がったところ michi o magatta tokoro

arrivals (airport) 到着 toochaku

arrive v 着きます tsuki masu

artery 動脈 doomyaku

arthritis 関節炎 kansetsuen

Asian アジアの ajia no

aspirin 頭痛薬 zutsuuyaku

asthmatic 喘息の zensoku no

ATM キャッシュコーナー kyasshu koonaa

attack v 襲います osoimasu

attend v 出席します shusseki shimasu

attraction (place) アトラクション atorakushon

attractive 魅力的 miryokuteki

Australian オーストラリア人 oosutorariajin

automatic 自動 jidoo

automatic car オートマチック ootomachikku

B

baby 赤ちゃん akachan

baby bottle 哺乳瓶 honyuubin

baby wipe おしりふき oshirifuki

babysitter ベビーシッター bebii shittaa

back (body part) 背中 senaka

backpack リュックサック ryukkusakku

bag バッグ baggu

baggage [BE] 荷物 nimotsu

baggage claim 荷物引渡所 nimotsu hikiwatashijo

baggage ticket 荷物引換証 nimotsu hikikaeshoo

bakery パン屋 pan-ya

ballet バレエ baree

bandage 包帯 hootai

bank 銀行 ginkoo

bar バー baa

barber 床屋 tokoya

baseball 野球 yakyuu

basket (grocery store) かご kago

basketball バスケットボール basuketto booru

bathroom 風呂場 furoba

bathroom (toilet) トイレ toire

battery 電池 denchi

battleground 戦場跡 senjooato

beach 海岸/ビーチ kaigan/biichi

beautiful 美しい utsukushii

bed ベッド beddo

begin v 始めます hajime masu

before 前 mae

beginner 初心者 shoshinsha

behind 後ろ ushiro

beige ベージュ beeju

belt ベルト beruto

berth 寝台 shindai

best 一番いい ichiban ii

better もっといい motto ii

bicycle 自転車 jitensha

big 大きい ookii

bigger もっと大きい motto ookii

bike route 自転車ルート jitensha ruuto

bikini ビキニ bikini

bill v (charge) 請求します seekyuu shimasu; ~ n (money) 紙幣 shihee; ~ n (of sale) 請求書 seekyuusho; itemized ~ 明細書 meesaisho

bird 鳥 tori

birthday 誕生日 tanjoobi

black 黒い kuroi

bladder 膀胱 bookoo

bland 味が薄い aji ga usui

blanket 毛布 moofu

bleed v 出血します shukketsu shimasu

blood 血液 ketsueki

blood pressure 血圧 ketsuatsu

blouse ブラウス burausu

blue ブルー buruu

board v (plane) 搭乗します toojoo shimasu, (train) 乗車します joosha shimasu

boarding pass 搭乗券 toojoo ken

boat ボート booto

bone 骨 hone

book 本 hon

bookstore 本屋 hon-ya

boots ブーツ buutu

boring つまらない tsumaranai

botanical garden 植物園 shokubutsuen

bother v 邪魔します jama shimasu

bottle 瓶 bin

bottle opener 栓抜き sennuki

bowl ボール booru

box 箱 hako

boy 男の子 otoko noko

boyfriend ボーイフレンド booi furendo

bra ブラジャー burajaa

bracelet ブレスレット buresuretto

brakes (car) ブレーキ bureeki

break v 折れます oremasu

break-in (burglary) 侵入します shinnyuu shimasu
breakdown 故障 koshoo
breakfast 朝食 chooshoku
breast 乳房 chibusa
breastfeed 母乳をあげます bonyuu o agemasu
breathe v 呼吸します kokyuu shimasu
bridge 橋 hashi
briefs (clothing) ブリーフ buriifu
bring (people) v 連れてきます tsurete kimasu; **(things)** 持ってきます motte kimasu
British イギリス人 igirisujin
broken 壊れた kowareta
brooch ブローチ buroochi
broom 箒 hooki
brother (my older) 兄 ani
brother (my younger) 弟 otooto
brother (someone else's older) お兄さん oniisan
brother (someone else's younger) 弟さん otootosan
brown 茶色 chairo
bug 虫 mushi
building ビル/ 建物 biru/ tatemono
burn v 焼きます yakimasu
bus バス basu
bus station バスターミナル basu taaminaru

bus stop バス停留所 / バス停 basu teeryuujo/basutee
bus ticket バスの切符 basu no kippu
bus tour バス旅行 basu ryokoo
business 仕事 shigoto
business card 名刺 meeshi
business center ビジネス・センター bijinesu sentaa
business class ビジネス・クラス bijinesu kurasu
business hours 営業時間 eegyoo jikan
butcher 肉屋 nikuya
buttocks お尻 oshiri
buy v 買います kaimasu
bye ごめんください gomen kudasai

C

cabin キャビン kyabin
cable car ケーブル・カー keeburu kaa
café 喫茶店 kissaten
call v 電話します denwa shimasu
calligraphy supplies 習字用具 shuuji yoogu
calories カロリー karorii
camera カメラ kamera
camp v キャンプします kyanpu shimasu; **no ~ing** キャンプ禁止 kyanpu kinshi
campsite キャンプ場 kyanpujoo

can opener 缶切り kankiri

Canada カナダ kanada

Canadian カナダ人 kanadajin

cancel v キャンセルします kyanseru shimasu

candy キャンデー kyandee

canned good 缶詰 kanzume

canyon 峡谷 kyookoku

car 車 kuruma

car hire [BE] レンタカー rentakaa

car park [BE] 駐車場 chuushajoo

car rental レンタカー rentakaa

car seat チャイルドシート chairudo shiito

carafe カラフ karafu

card カード kaado

carry-on 手荷物 tenimotsu

cart カート kaato

carton カートン kaaton

case (amount) ケース keesu

cash v 換金します kankin shimasu; ~ n 現金 genkin

cash advance キャッシング・サービス kyasshingu saabisu

cashier 会計 kaikee

casino カジノ kajino

castle お城 oshiro

cathedral 大聖堂 daiseedoo

cave 洞窟 dookutsu

CD CD shii dii

cell phone 携帯電話 keetai denwa

Celsius 接氏 sesshi

centimeter センチメートル senchi-meetoru

chair 椅子 isu

chair lift スキーリフト sukii rifuto

change v (buses) 乗り換えます norikaemasu; ~ v (money) 替えます kaemasu; ~ v (baby) おむつを替えます omutsu o kaemasu; ~ n (plan) 変更 henkoo; ~ n (money) お釣り otsuri

charcoal 炭 sumi

charge v (credit card) カードで払います kaado de haraimasu; n (cost) 料金 ryookin

cheap 安い yasui

cheaper もっと安い motto yasui

check v (something) 調べます shirabemasu; ~ v (luggage) 預けます azukemasu; ~ n (payment) お勘定 okanjoo

check-in チェックイン chekku in

checking account 当座預金口座 tooza yoking kooza

check-out (hotel) n チェックアウト chekku auto

chemical toilet ケミカルトイレ kemikaru toire

chemist [BE] 薬局 yakkyoku

cheque [BE] チェック chekku

chest (body part) 胸 mune

chest pain 胸の痛み mune no itami
chewing gum ガム gamu
child 子供 kodomo
child's seat 子供用の椅子 kodomoyoo no isu
children's menu 子供用のメニュー kodomoyoo no menyuu
children's portion 子供用のメニュー kodomoyoo no menyuu
china 瀬戸物 setomono
China 中国 chuugoku
Chinese (language) 中国語 chuugokugo
Chinese (people) 中国人 chuugokujin
chopsticks おはし ohashi
church 教会 kyookai
cigar 葉巻 hamaki
cigarette 煙草 tabako
class クラス kurasu
clay pot 土器 doki
classical music クラシック音楽 kurashikku ongaku
clean v きれいにします kirei ni shimasu; ~ adj きれい kiree
cleaning product 洗浄剤 senjoozai
cleaning supplies クリーニング用品 kuriiningu yoohin
clear v (on an ATM) 消去します shookyo shimasu
cliff 崖 gake

cling film [BE] ラップ rappu
close v (a shop) 閉めます shimemasu; ~ adj 近い chikai
closed 閉館 heekan
clothing 衣類 irui
clothing store 洋服屋 yoofukuya
club クラブ kurabu
coat コート kooto
coffee shop 喫茶店 kissaten
coin 硬貨 kooka
cold (sickness) 風邪 kaze; ~ (weather) 寒い samui; ~ (food) 冷たい tsumetai
colleague 同僚 dooryoo
cologne オーデコロン oodekoron
color 色 iro
comb 櫛 kushi
come v 来ます kimasu
complaint 苦情 kujoo
computer コンピュータ konpyuuta
concert コンサート konsaato
concert hall コンサートホール konsaato hooru
condition (medical) 症状 shoojoo
conditioner コンディショナー kondishonaa
condom コンドーム kondoomu
conference 会議 kaigi
confirm v 確認します kakunin shimasu
congestion 混雑 konzatsu

connect v (internet) 接続します setsuzoku shimasu

connection (internet) 接続 setsuzoku; ~ (flight) 連絡 renraku

constipated 便秘 benpi

consulate 領事館 ryoojikan

consultant コンサルタント konsarutanto

contact v 連絡します renraku shimasu

contact lens コンタクトレンズ kontakuto renzu; ~ solution コンタクトレンズ液 kontakuto renzu eki

contagious 伝染性 densensee

convention hall 会議場 kaigijoo

conveyor belt コンベヤーベルト konbeyaa beruto

cook v 料理します ryoori shimasu

cooking gas ガス gasu

cool (temperature) 涼しい suzushii

copper 銅 doo

corkscrew コルクスクリュー koruku sukuryuu

cost v かかります kakarimasu

cot 折り畳みベッド oritatami beddo

cotton 綿／コットン men/ kotton

cough 咳 seki

country code 国番号 kuni bangoo

cover charge カバーチャージ kabaa chaaji

crash v (car) ぶつかります butsukarimasu

cream (ointment) 軟膏 nankoo

credit card クレジットカード kurejitto kaado

crew neck クルーネック kuruu nekku

crib ベビーベッド bebii beddo

crystal 水晶 suishoo

cup カップ kappu

currency 通貨 tsuuka

currency exchange 両替 ryoogae; ~ office 両替所 ryoogaejo

current account [BE] 当座預金 tooza yokin

customs 税関 zeekan

cut v (hair) カットします katto shimasu

cut n (injury) 傷 kizu

cute 可愛い kawaii

cycling サイクリング saikuringu

D

damage v 壊れます kowaremasu

damaged 壊れた kowareta

dance v 踊ります odorimasu

dance club ダンスクラブ dansu kurabu

dangerous 危ない abunai

dark 暗い kurai

date (calendar) 日付け hizuke

day 日 hi

deaf 耳が聞こえない mimi ga kikoenai

debit card デビットカード debitto kaado

deck chair デッキチェア dekki chea

declare v 申告します shisnkoku shimasu

decline v (credit card) 拒否します kyohi shimasu

deeply 深く fukaku

degrees (temperature) 度 do

delay v 遅れます okuremasu

delete v 削除します sakujo shimasu

delicatessen デリカテッセン derikatessen

delicious おいしい oishii

denim デニム denimu

dentist 歯医者 haisha

denture 入れ歯 ireba

deodorant デオドラント deodoranto

department store デパート depaato

departure 出発 shuppatsu

deposit v 預けます azukemasu; ~ n (security) 前金 maekin

desert 砂漠 sabaku

detergent 洗剤 senzai

diabetic 糖尿病 toonyoobyoo

dial v 電話をかけます denwa o kakemasu

diamond ダイアモンド daiamondo

diaper おむつ omutsu

diarrhea 下痢 geri

diesel ディーゼル diizeru

difficult 難しい muzukashii

digital デジタル dejitaru; ~ camera デジタルカメラ dejitaru kamera; ~ photo デジタル写真 dejitaru shashin ~ print デジタルカメラプリント dejitaru kamera purinto

dining room 食堂 shokudoo

dinner 食事 shokuji

direction 方向 hookoo

dirty 汚い kitanai

disabled 身体障害者 shintai shoogaisha; ~ accessible [BE] バリアフリー設備 baria furii setsubi

disconnect (computer) 接続を切ります setsuzoku o kirimasu

discount 割引 waribiki

dish (kitchen) 食器 shokki

dishwasher 食洗器 shokusen ki

dishwashing liquid 中性洗剤 chuusee senzai

display 表示 hyooji

display case ショーケース shookeesu

disposable 使い捨て tsukaisute

disposable razor 使い捨てカミソリ tsukaisute kamisori

dive v 飛び込みます tobikomimasu

diving equipment 潜水用具 sensui yoogu

divorce v 離婚します rikon shimasu

dizzy めまいがします memai ga shimasu

doctor 医者 isha

doll 人形 ningyoo

dollar (U.S.) ドル doru

domestic 国内の kokunai no

domestic flight 国内線 kokunaisen

dormitory 寮 ryoo

double bed ダブルベッド daburu beddo

downtown 繁華街 hankagai

dozen ダース daasu

drag lift 抗力浮揚 kooryoku fuyoo

dress (piece of clothing) ワンピース wanpiisu

dress code 服装規定 fukusoo kitee

drink v 飲みます nomimasu; ~ n 飲み物 nomimono

drink menu ドリンクメニュー dorinku menyuu

drinking water 飲料水 inryoosui

drive v 運転します unten shimasu

driver's license 運転免許証 unten menkyoshoo; ~ **number** 運転免許証番号 unten menkyoshoo bangoo

drop (medicine) 一滴 itteki

drowsiness 眠気 nemuke

dry cleaner ドライクリーニング店 dorai kuriiningu ten

during …の間 …no aida

duty (tax) 関税 kanzee

duty-free 免税 menzee

DVD DVD dii bui dii

E

ear 耳 mimi

earache 耳の痛み mimi no itami

early 早い hayai

earrings イヤリング iyaringu

east 東 higashi

easy やさしい yasashii

eat v 食べます tabeamasu

economy class エコノミークラス ekonomii kurasu

elbow 肘 hiji

electric outlet コンセント konsento

elevator エレベーター erebeetaa

e-mail v メールします meeru shimasu; ~ n 電子メール denshi meeru

e-mail address 電子メールアドレス denshi meeru adoresu

emergency 緊急 kinkyuu

emergency exit 非常口 hijoo guchi

empty v 空にします kara ni shimasu

end v 終わります owarimasu

English (language) 英語 eego

English (people) イギリス人 igirisujin

engrave v 彫り込みます horikomimasu

enjoy v 楽しみます tanoshimimasu

enter v 入ります hairimasu; (computer) 入力します nyuuryoku shimasu

entertainment エンターテインメント entaateenmento

entrance 入口 iriguchi

envelope 封筒 fuutoo

equipment 道具 doogu

escalator エスカレーター esukareetaa

e-ticket Eチケット i chiketto

evening 夕方 yuugata

excess 超過 chooka

exchange v (money) 両替します ryoogae shimasu; ~ v (goods) 取り替えます torikaemasu; ~ n (place) 交換所 kookanjo

exchange rate (為替)レート (kawase) reeto

excursion エクスカーション ekusukaashon

excuse v 許します yurushimasu

exhausted 疲れている tsukareteiru

exit v 出ます demasu; ~ n 出口 deguchi

expensive 高い takai

expert (skill level) 専門家 senmonka

exposure (film) …枚撮り …maitori

express (mail) 速達 sokutatsu; (train) 急行 kyuukoo

extension (phone) 内線 naisen

extra 特別な tokubetsuna

extra large 特大 tokudai

extract v (tooth) 抜きます nukimasu

eye 目 me

F

face 顔 kao

facial フェーシャル feesharu

family 家族 kazoku

fan (appliance) 扇風機 senpuuki

far 遠い tooi

far-sighted 遠視の enshi no

farm 農家 nooka

fast 速い hayai

fast food ファーストフード faasuto fuudo

fat free 無脂肪 mushiboo

father (one's own) 父 chichi; **(someone else's)** お父さん otoosan

fax v ファックスします fakkusu shimasu; ~ n ファックス fakkusu

fax number ファックス番号 fakkusu bangoo

fee 費用 hiyoo

feed v 授乳します junyuu shimasu

ferry フェリー ferii

fever 熱 netsu

field (sports) フィールド fiirudo

fill up v (food) 満タンにします mantan ni shimasu

fill out v (form) 記入します kinyuu shimasu

filling (tooth) 詰物 tsumemono

film (camera) フィルム fuirumu

fine (fee) 罰金 bakkin

finger 指 yubi

fingernail 爪 tsume

fire 火 hi

fire department 消防署 shooboosho

fire door 耐火扉 taika tobira

first 最初の saisho no

first class ファーストクラス faasuto kurasu

fish 魚 sakana

fit (clothing) 合います aimasu

fitting room 試着室 shichakushitsu

fix v (repair) 直します naoshimasu

flashlight 懐中電灯 kaichuu dentoo

flight 便 bin

floor 階 kai

flower 花 hana

folk music フォークミュージック fooku myuujikku

food 食物 tabemono

foot 足 ashi

football game [BE] サッカーゲーム sakkaa geemu

for (a day) 一日間 ichiinichiikan

forecast 予報 yohoo

foreigner 外国人 gaikokujin

forest 森 mori

fork フォーク fooku

form (fill-in) 用紙 yooshi

formula (baby) フォーミュラ foomyura

fountain 噴水 funsui

free (not busy) 暇 hima; ~ **(available)** 空いています aiteimasu;

free (no charge) 無料 muryoo

freezer 冷凍庫 reetooko

fresh 新しい atarashii

friend 友人 yuujin

frying pan フライパン furaipan

full-service 完全サービス
  kanzen saabisu

G

game ゲーム geemu
garage 修理工場 shuurikoojoo
garbage bag ごみ袋
  gomibukuro
gas ガソリン gasorin
gas station ガソリンスタンド
  gasorin sutando
gate (airport) ゲート geeto
gay bar ゲイバー gei baa
gay club ゲイクラブ gei kurabu
gel (hair) ジェル jeru
get to 着きます tsukimasu
get off (a train/bus/subway)
  下ります orimasu
gift 贈り物 okurimono
gift shop 売店 baiten
girl 女の子 onna no ko
girlfriend ガールフレンド
  gaaru furendo
give v あげます agemasu
glass (drinking) コップ koppu;
  ~ (material) ガラス garasu
glasses 眼鏡 megane
go v (somewhere) 行きます
  ikimasu
gold 金 kin
golf course ゴルフ場 gorufujoo
golf tournament ゴルフトーナ
  メント gorufu toonamento
good 良い ii; (food) おいしい
  oishii

good afternoon こんにちは
  konnichiwa
good evening 今晩は
  konbanwa
good morning お早うございま
  す ohayoo gozaimasu
goodbye さようなら sayoonara
gram グラム guramu
grandchild 孫 mago
grandparent (one's own)
  祖父/祖母 sofu/sobo;
  (someone else's) おじい
  さん／おばあさん ojiisan/
  obaasan
gray グレー guree
green 緑／グリーン midori/
  guriin
grocery store 食料品店
  shokuryoohinten
ground floor 一階 ikkai
group グループ guruupu
guide n ガイド gaido
guide book ガイドブック gaido
  bukku
guide dog 盲導犬 moodoo ken
gym トレーニングジム
  toreeningu jimu
gynecologist 婦人科医
  fujinkai

H

hair 髪 kami
hair dryer ヘアドライヤー hea
  doraiyaa
hair salon 美容院 biyooin

hairbrush ヘアブラシ hea burashi

haircut ヘアカット hea katto

hairspray ヘアスプレー hea supuree

hairstyle ヘアスタイル hea sutairu

hairstylist ヘアスタイリスト hea sutairisuto

half 半分 hanbun

half hour 半時間 han jikan

half-kilo 半キロ han kiro

hammer ハンマー hanmaa

hand 手 te

hand luggage [BE] 手荷物 tenimotsu

handbag [BE] ハンドバッグ hando baggu

handicapped 身体障害者 shintai shoogaisha

handicapped-accessible ハンディキャップ用 handikyappuyoo

hangover 二日酔い futsuka yoi

happy 楽しい tanoshii

hat 帽子 booshi

have v あります arimasu

head (body part) 頭 atama

headache 頭痛 zutsuu

headphones ヘッドフォン heddofon

health 健康 kenkoo

health food store 健康食品店 kenkoo shokuhinten

heart 心臓 shinzoo

heart condition 心臓病 shinzoobyoo

heat 熱 netsu

heater 暖房 danboo

heating [BE] ヒーター／暖房 hiitaa/danboo

hello こんにちは konnichiwa; (on the phone) もしもし moshi moshi

helmet ヘルメット herumetto

help 助け tasuke

here ここ koko

hi どうも doomo

high 高い takai

highchair ハイチェアー haicheaa

highway ハイウェー haiuee

hill 丘 oka

hire v [BE] 借ります karimasu

hire car [BE] レンタカー rentakaa

hitchhike v ヒッチハイクします hitchi haiku shimasu

hockey ホッケー hokkee

holiday [BE] 休日 kyuujitsu

horse track 競馬場 keebajoo

hospital 病院 byooin

hostel ホステル hosuteru

hot (temperature) 暑い atsui; ~ (spicy) 辛い karai

hot spring 温泉 onsen

hot water お湯 oyu

hotel ホテル hoteru

hour 時間 jikan

house 家 ie

household good 家庭用品
katee yoohin

housekeeping services 客室
清掃サービス kyakushitsu
seesoo saabisu

how どうやって dooyatte

how much (money) いくら
ikura; (quantity) どのくらい
dono kurai

hungry お腹がすいた
onaka ga suita

hurt 痛い itai

husband (one's own) 主人
shujin;
(some one else's) ご主人
goshujin

I

ibuprofen イブプロフェン
ibupurofen

ice 氷 koori

ice hockey アイスホッケー aisu
hokkee

icy 氷の koori no

identification 身分証明 mibun
shoomee

ill 病気 byooki

include v 含みます
fukumimasu

indoor pool 室内プール
shitsunai puuru

inexpensive 安い yasui

infected 感染した kansen
shita

information (phone) 案内
annai

information desk 受付
uketsuke

inn 旅館 ryokan

insect bite 虫さされ mushi
sasare

insect repellent 虫除け mushi
yoke

insert v (on an ATM) 挿入し
ます／入れます soonyuu
shimasu/iremasu

insomnia 不眠症 fuminshoo

instant message インスタ
ント・メッセージ insutanto
messeeji

insulin インスリン insurin

insurance 保険 hoken; v
保険を掛けます hoken o
kakemasu

insurance card 保険証
hokenshoo

insurance company 保険会社
hoken gaisha

interesting 面白い omoshiroi

international (airport area)
国際 kokusai

international flight 国際線
kokusaisen

international student
card 国際学生証 kokusai
gakuseishoo

internet インターネット
intaanetto

internet cafe インターネットカフェ intaanetto kafe

internet service インターネットサービス intaanetto saabisu

interpreter 通訳者 tsuuyakusha

intersection 交差点 koosaten

intestine 腸 choo

introduce v 紹介します shookai shimasu

invoice 請求書 seekyuusho

Ireland アイルランド airurando

Irish アイルランド人 airurando jin

iron v アイロンをかけます airon o kakemasu; ~ n アイロン airon

J

jacket ジャケット jaketto

Japanese (people) 日本人 nihonjin

Japanese (language) 日本語 nihongo

jar 瓶 bin

jaw 顎 ago

jazz ジャズ jazu

jazz club ジャズクラブ jazu kurabu

jeans ジーパン／ジーンズ jiipan/jiinzu

jeweler 宝石店 hoosekiten

jewelry 宝石 hooseki

join v 加入します kanyuu shimasu

joint (body part) 関節 kansetsu

K

key 鍵 kagi

key card キーカード kii kaado

key ring キーホルダー kii horudaa

kiddie pool 子供用プール kodomoyoo puuru

kidney (body part) 腎臓 jinzoo

kilogram キロ(グラム) kiro (guramu)

kilometer キロ(メートル) kiro (meetoru)

kiss v キスします kisu shimasu

kitchen 台所 daidokoro; ~ foil [BE] アルミフォイル arumifoiru

knee 膝 hiza

knife ナイフ naifu

L

lace レース reesu

lacquerware 漆器 shikki

lactose intolerant 乳糖不耐症 nyuutoo futaishoo

lake 湖 mizuumi

large 大きい ookii

last 最後 saigo

late (time) 遅い osoi

later あとで atode

launderette [BE] コインランドリー koin randorii

laundromat コインランドリー koin randorii

laundry 洗濯 sentaku

laundry facility 洗濯施設 sentaku shisetsu

laundry service ランドリーサービス randorii saabisu

lawyer 弁護士 bengoshi

leather 皮 kawa

leave v 出ます demasu

left (direction) 左 hidari

leg 脚 ashi

lens レンズ renzu

less もっと少ない motto sukunai

lesson レッスン ressun

letter 手紙 tegami

library 図書館 toshokan

life boat 救命ボート kyuumee booto

life jacket 救命胴衣 kyuumee dooi

lifeguard ライフガード raifu gaado

lift リフト rifuto; ~ [BE] エレベーター erebeetaa

lift pass リフト券 rifuto ken

light (overhead) 電灯 dentoo; ~ v (cigarette) 火をつけます hi o tsukemasu

lightbulb 電球 denkyuu

lighter ライター raitaa

like v 好きです sukidesu

line (train) 線 sen

linen 麻 asa

lip 唇 kuchibiru

liquor store 酒屋 sakaya

liter リットル rittoru

little 少し／ちょっと sukoshi/chotto

live v 住みます sumimasu

liver (body part) 肝臓 kanzoo

loafers ローファー roofaa

local 地方 chihoo

lock v 鍵をかけます kagi o kakemasu; ~ n 鍵 kagi

locker ロッカー rokkaa

log on ログオンします roggu on shimasu

log off ログオフします roggu ofu shimasu

long 長い nagai

long sleeves 長袖 nagasode

long-sighted [BE] 遠視 enshi

look v 見ます mimasu

lose v (something) なくします nakushimasu

lost 道に迷いました michi ni mayoi mashita

lost and found お忘れ物承り所 owasure mono uketamawari jo

lotion ローション rooshon

louder もっと大きい声で motto ookii koe de

love 愛 ai

low 低い hikui

luggage 荷物 nimotsu

luggage cart カート kaato

luggage locker コインロッカー koin rokkaa

luggage ticket 荷物引換券 nimotsu hikikae ken

lunch 昼食 chuushoku

lung 肺 hai

M

magazine 雑誌 zasshi

magnificent 立派 rippa

mail v 郵送します yuusoo shimasu; ~ n 手紙 tegami

mailbox 郵便ポスト yuubin posuto

main attraction メインイベント mein ibento

main course メインコース mein koosu

make up a prescription [BE] 調合します choogoo shimasu

mall ショッピングモール shoppingu mooru

man 男の人 otoko no hito

manager (restaurant, hotel) 支配人 shihainin; (shop) 店長 tenchoo

manicure マニキュア manikyua

manual car マニュアル manyuaru

map n 地図 chizu

market マーケット maaketto

married 結婚している kekkon shiteiru

marry v 結婚します kekkon shimasu

mass (church service) ミサ misa

massage マッサージ massaaji

match n 試合 shiai

meal 食事 shokuji

measure v (someone) 測ります hakarimasu

measuring cup 計量カップ keeryoo kappu

measuring spoon 計量スプーン keeryoo supuun

mechanic 修理工 shuurikoo

medicine 薬 kusuri

medium (size) 中ぐらい chuugurai

meet v (someone) 待ち合わせす machiawasemasu

meeting 会議 kaigi

meeting room 会議室 kaigishitsu

membership card 会員証 kaiin shoo

memorial (place) 記念館 kinenkan

memory card メモリーカード memorii kaado

mend v 直します naoshimasu

menstrual cramp 生理痛 seiritsuu

menu メニュー menyuu

message メッセージ、ご伝言 messeeji, godengon

meter (parking) 料金メーター ryookin meetaa

microwave 電子レンジ denshi renji

midday *[BE]* 昼間 hiruma

midnight 真夜中 mayonaka

mileage 距離 kyori

mini-bar ミニバー mini baa

minute 分 fun/pun

missing いなくなる inakunaru

mistake 間違い machigai

mobile phone *[BE]* 携帯電話 keetai denwa

mobility 移動性 idoosee

money お金 okane

month 月 tsuki

mop モップ moppu

moped モペット mopetto

more もっと motto

morning 朝 asa

mosque 回教寺院 kaikyoo jiin

mother (one's own) 母 haha; **(some one else's)** お母さん okaasan

motion sickness 乗物酔い norimono yoi

motor boat モーターボート mootaa booto

motorcycle オートバイ ootobai

motorway *[BE]* 高速道路 koosoku dooro

mountain 山 yama

mountain bike マウンテンバイク maunten baiku

mousse (hair) ムース muusu

mouth 口 kuchi

movie 映画 eega

movie theater 映画館 eegakan

mug *v* 襲います osoimasu

muscle 筋肉 kinniku

museum 博物館 hakubutsukan

music 音楽 ongaku

music store 楽器屋 gakkiya

N

nail file ネイルファイル neeru fairu

nail salon ネイルサロン neeru saron

name 名前 namae

napkin ナプキン napukin

nappy *[BE]* おむつ omutsu

nationality 国籍 kokuseki

nature preserve 自然保護区 shizen hogoku

nauseous 吐き気 hakike

near 近く chikaku

near-sighted 近視 kinshi

nearby 近く chikaku

neck 首 kubi

necklace ネックレス nekkuresu

need *v* 要ります irimasu

newspaper 新聞 shinbun

newsstand キオスク kiosuku

next 次 tsugi

nice すてき suteki

night 夜 yoru

nightclub ナイトクラブ naito
  kurabu
no いいえ iie
non-alcoholic ノンアルコール
  non arukooru
non-smoking 禁煙 kin-en
noon 正午 shoogo
north 北 kita
nose 鼻 hana
note [BE] お札 osatsu
notify v 知らせます
  shirasemasu
novice (skill level) 初心者
  shoshinsha
now 今 ima
number 数字 suuji
nurse 看護士 kangoshi

O

office オフィス ofisu
office hours オフィスアワー
  ofisu awaa
off-licence [BE] 酒屋 sakaya
oil オイル oiru
OK オーケー ookee
old (person) 年寄り toshiyori;
  (thing) 古い furui
on the corner 角の kadono
once 一度 ichido
one 一つ hitotsu
one-way (ticket) 片道
  katamichi
one-way street 一方通行
  ippoo tsuukoo
only ただ tada

open v 開けます akemasu; ~
  adj 開いている aiteiru
opera オペラ opera
opera house オペラハウス
  opera hausu
opposite 向かい mukai
optician 眼鏡店 meganeten
orange (color) オレンジ色
  orenji iro
orchestra オーケストラ
  ookesutora
order v 注文します chuumon
  shimasu
outdoor pool 屋外プール
  okugai puuru
outside 外 soto
over the counter
  (medication)
  処方箋無し shohoosen nashi
overdone 焼き過ぎ yakisugi
overlook (scenic place)
  見晴し台 miharashidai
overnight 夜通し yodooshi
oxygen treatment 酸素治療
  sanso chiryoo

P

p.m. n 午後 gogo (1 p.m.; gogo
  ichiji)
pacifier おしゃぶり oshaburi
pack v 詰めます tsumemasu
package 小包 kozutsumi
paddling pool [BE] 子供用プー
  ル kodomoyoo puuru

pad *[BE]* 生理用ナプキン
seeriyoo napukin

pain 痛み itami

pajamas パジャマ pajama

palace 宮殿 kyuuden

pants ズボン zubon

pantyhose パンスト pansuto

paper 紙 kami

paper towel ペーパータオル
peepaa taoru

paracetamol *[BE]* アセタミノー
フェン asetaminoofen

park *v* 駐車します chuusha
shimasu; ~ *n* 公園 kooen

parking garage 駐車場
chuushajoo

parking lot 駐車場 chuushajoo

parking meter 料金メーター
ryookin meetaa

part (for car) 部品 buhin

part-time パートタイム paato
taimu

passenger 乗客 jookyaku

passport パスポート
pasupooto

passport control 入国手続き
nyuukoku tetsuzuki

password パスワード pasu
waado

pastry shop ケーキ屋 keekiya

path 道路 dooro

pay *v* 払います haraimasu

pay phone 公衆電話 kooshuu
denwa

peak (of a mountain) 山頂
sanchoo

pearl 真珠 shinju

pedestrian 歩行者 hokoosha

pediatrician 小児科医
shoonikai

pedicure ペディキュア
pedikyua

pen ペン pen

penicillin ペニシリン penishirin

penis ペニス penisu

per につき nitsuki

per day 一日につき ichinichi
ni tsuki

per hour 一時間につき
ichijikan ni tsuki

per night 一晩につき hitoban
ni tsuki

per week 一週間につき
isshuukan ni tsuki

perfume 香水 koosui

period (menstrual) 生理 seeri;
~(of time) 期間 kikan

permit *v* 許可します kyoka
shimasu

petite ペティート petiito

petrol *[BE]* ガソリン gasorin

petrol station *[BE]* ガソリンス
タンド gasorin sutando

pharmacy 薬局 yakkyoku

phone *v* 電話します denwa
shimasu; ~ *n* 電話 denwa

phone call 電話 denwa

phone card テレホンカード
terehon kaado

phone number 電話番号 denwa bangoo

photo 写真 shashin

photocopy コピー kopii

photography 写真撮影 shashin satsuee

pick up (something) 受け取ります uketorimasu

picnic area ピクニック場 pikunikkujoo

pill (birth control) ピル piru

pillow 枕 makura

personal identification number (PIN) 暗証番号 anshoo bangoo

pink ピンク pinku

piste *[BE]* ゲレンデ gerende

piste map *[BE]* ゲレンデ地図 gerende chizu

pizzeria ピザ・レストラン piza resutoran

place *v* **(a bet)** 掛け金を払います kakekin o haraimasu; *n* 場所 basho

plane 飛行機 hikooki

plastic wrap ラップ rappu

plate 皿 sara

platform ホーム hoomu

platinum プラチナ purachina

play *v* します shimasu; ~ *n* **(theatre)** 芝居 shibai

playground 公園 kooen

playpen ベビーサークル bebii saakuru

please (asking for a favor) お願いします onegai shimasu; **(offering a favor)** どうぞ doozo

pleasure 楽しみ tanoshimi

plunger トイレの吸引具 toire no kyuuingu

plus size プラスサイズ purasu saizu

pocket ポケット poketto

poison 毒 doku

poles (skiing) ストック sutokku

police 警察 keesatsu

police report 警察の証明書 keesatsu no shoomeesho

police station 交番 kooban

pond 池 ike

pool プール puuru

pop music ポピュラー音楽 popyuraa ongaku

portion 部分 bubun

post *[BE]* 手紙 tegami

post office 郵便局 yuubinkyoku

postbox *[BE]* 郵便ポスト yuubin posuto

postcard 葉書 hagaki

pot 深鍋 fukanabe

pottery 陶器 tooki

pound (weight) ポンド pondo; **~ (British sterling)** ポンド pondo

pregnant 妊娠 ninshin

prepaid phone プリペイド携帯 puripeedo keetai

prescribe v 処方します shohoo shimasu

prescription 処方箋 shohoosen

press v (clothing) アイロンをかけます airon o kakemasu

price 値段 nedan

print v 印刷します insatsu shimasu

problem 問題 mondai

produce 食料品 shokuryoohin

produce store 食料品店 shokuryoohinten

prohibit v 禁止します kinshi shimasu

pronounce v 発音します hatsuon shimasu

public 公共 kookyoo

pull v 引きます hikimasu

purple 紫 murasaki

purse 財布 saifu

push v 押します oshimasu

pushchair [BE] ベビーカー bebii kaa

Q

quality 質 shitsu

question 質問 shitsumon

quiet 静か shizuka

R

racetrack 競馬場 keebajoo

racket (sports) ラケット raketto

railway station [BE] 駅 eki

rain n 雨 ame

raincoat レインコート reinkooto

rainforest 雨林 urin

rainy 雨の ameno

rap (music) ラップ rappu

rape 強姦 gookan

rash 発疹 hasshin

razor blade カミソリの刃 kamisori no ha

reach v 届きます todokimasu

ready 用意ができている yooi ga dekite iru

real 本物 honmono

receipt レシート／領収書 reshiito/ryooshuusho

receive v 受け取ります uketorimasu

reception 受付 uketsuke

recharge v 充電します juuden shimasu

recommend v 推薦します suisen shimasu

recommendation 推薦 suisen

recycling リサイクリング risaikuringu

red 赤い akai

refrigerator 冷蔵庫 reezooko

region 地域 chiiki

registered mail 書留 kakitome

regular レギュラー regyuraa

relationship 関係 kankee

rent v 借ります karimasu

rental car レンタカー rentakaa

repair v 修理します shuuri shimasu

repeat v もう一度言います moo ichido iimasu

reservation 予約 yoyaku

reservation desk 予約窓口 yoyaku madoguchi

reserve v 予約します yoyaku shimasu

restaurant レストラン resutoran

restroom 化粧室 keshooshitsu

retired 退職した taishoku shita

return v 返します kaeshimasu; ~ n [BE] 往復 oofuku

rib (body part) 肋骨 rokkotsu

rice cooker 炊飯器 suihanki

right (direction) 右 migi

right of way 優先権 yuusenken

ring 指輪／リング yubiwa/ringu

river 川 kawa

road map 道路地図 dooro chizu

rob v 盗みます nusumimasu

robbed 盗まれました nusumare mashita

romantic ロマンチック romanchikku

room 部屋 heya

room key 部屋の鍵 heya no kagi

room service ルームサービス ruumu saabisu

round-trip 往復 oofuku

route コース koosu

rowboat ボート booto

rubbish [BE] ゴミ gomi

rubbish bag [BE] ゴミ袋 gomi bukuro

ruins 遺跡 iseki

rush ラッシュ rasshu

S

sad 悲しい kanashii

safe (thing) 金庫 kinko; ~ (protected) 安全 anzen

sales tax 消費税 shoohizee

sandals サンダル sandaru

sanitary napkin 生理用ナプキン seeriyoo napukin

saucepan 鍋 nabe

sauna サウナ sauna

save v (on a computer) 保存します hozon shimasu

savings (account) 普通預金 futsuu yokin

scanner スキャナー sukyanaa

scarf スカーフ sukaafu

schedule v 予定に入れます yotee ni iremasu; ~ n 予定 yotee

school 学校 gakkoo

science 科学 kagaku

scissors はさみ hasami

sea 海 umi

seat 席 seki

security 警備 keebi

see v 見ます mimasu

self-service セルフサービス serufu saabisu

sell *v* 売ります urimasu

send *v* 送ります okurimasu

senior citizen 高齢者 kooreesha

separated (marriage) 別居 bekkyo

serious 真面目な majimena

service (in a restaurant) サービス saabisu

sexually transmitted disease (STD) 性病 seebyoo

shampoo シャンプー shanpuu

sharp 鋭い surudoi

shaving cream シェービングクリーム sheebingu kuriimu

sheet シーツ shiitsu

ship *v* (mail) 送ります okurimasu

shirt シャツ shatsu

shoe store 靴屋 kutsuya

shoes 靴 kutsu

shop *v* 買い物をします kaimono o shimasu

shopping 買い物 kaimono

shopping area 商店街 shooten gai

shopping centre *[BE]* ショッピングセンター shoppingu sentaa

shopping mall ショッピングモール shoppingu mooru

short 短い mijikai

short sleeves 半袖 hansode

shorts 半ズボン hanzubon

short-sighted *[BE]* 近視 kinshi

shoulder 肩 kata

show *v* 見せます misemasu

shower シャワー shawaa

shrine 神社 jinja

sick 病気 byooki

side dish 付け合わせ tsukeawase

side effect 副作用 fukusayoo

sightseeing 観光 kankoo

sightseeing tour 観光ツアー kankoo tsuaa

sign *v* 署名します／サインします shomeeshimasu/sainshimasu

silk 絹 kinu

silver 銀 gin

single (unmarried) 独身 dokushin

single bed シングルベッド shinguru beddo

single room シングルルーム shinguru ruumu

sink 流し nagashi

sister (my older) 姉 ane

sister (my younger) 妹 imooto

sister (someone else's older) お姉さん oneesan

sister (someone else's younger) 妹さん imootosan

sit *v* 座ります suwarimasu

size サイズ saizu

skin 皮膚 hifu

skirt スカート sukaato

ski スキー sukii

ski lift スキーリフト sukii rifuto

sleep v 眠ります nemurimasu

sleeper car 寝台車 shindaisha

sleeping bag 寝袋／スリーピングバッグ nebukuro/ suriipingu baggu

slice (of something) 一切れ hitokire

slippers スリッパ surippa

slower もっとゆっくり motto yukkuri

slowly ゆっくり yukkuri

small 小さい chiisai

smaller もっと小さい motto chiisai

smoke v 煙草を吸います tabako o suimasu

smoking (area) 喫煙席 kitsuenseki

snack bar スナックバー sunakku baa

sneaker スニーカー suniikaa

snorkeling equipment スノーケル用具 sunookeru yoogu

snowboard スノーボード sunoo boodo

snowshoe 雪靴 yukigutsu

snowy 雪の多い yuki no ooi

soap 石鹸 sekken

soccer サッカー sakkaa

sock 靴下 kutsushita

soother [BE] おしゃぶり oshaburi

sore throat 喉の痛み nodo no itami

sorry ごめんなさい gomennasai

south 南 minami

souvenir お土産 omiyage

souvenir store お土産屋 omiyageya

spa 温泉 onsen

spatula へら hera

speak v 話します hanashimasu

specialist (doctor) 専門医 senmon-i

specimen 見本 mihon

speeding スピード違反 supiido ihan

spell v つづりを言います tsuzuri o iimasu

spicy 辛い karai

spine (body part) 脊椎 sekitsui

spoon スプーン supuun

sports スポーツ supootsu

sporting goods store スポーツ用品店 supootsu yoohinten

sprain 捻挫 nenza

stadium スタジアム sutajiamu

stairs 階段 kaidan

stamp n (postage) 切手 kitte

start v (a car) スタートします sutaato shimasu

starter [BE] 前菜 zensai

station 駅 eki

statue 銅像 doozoo

stay v 泊まります tomarimasu

steal v 盗みます nusumimasu

steep 急斜面 kyuushamen

sterling silver 純銀 jungin

sting n 虫さされ mushi sasare

stolen 盗まれた nusumareta

stomach 胃 i

stomachache 腹痛 fukutsuu

stop v 止まります tomarimasu;
~ (bus) n バス停 basu tee

store directory 店内の案内
tennai no annai

storey [BE] 階 kai

stove コンロ konro

straight 真っ直ぐ massugu

strange 変 hen

stream 小川 ogawa

...Street ...通り ...doori

stroller ベビーカー bebiikaa

student 学生 gakusee

study v 勉強します benkyoo
shimasu

stunning 驚くほどの odoroku
hodono

subtitle (movie) 字幕 jimaku

subway 地下鉄 chikatetsu

subway station 地下鉄の駅
chikatetsu no eki

suit スーツ suutsu

suitcase スーツケース suutsu
keesu

sun 太陽 taiyoo

sunblock 日焼け止めクリーム
hiyakedome kuriimu

sunburn 日焼け hiyake

sunglasses サングラス
sangurasu

sunny 晴れの hareno

sunscreen 日除け hiyoke

sunstroke 日射病 nisshabyoo

super (fuel) スーパー suupaa

supermarket スーパー
suupaa

surfboard サーフボード saafu
boodo

sushi restaurant 寿司屋
sushi ya

swallow v 呑み込みます
nomikomimasu

sweater セーター seetaa

sweatshirt トレーナー
toreenaa

sweet (taste) 甘い amai

sweets [BE] キャンデー
kyandee

swelling 腫れ hare

swim v 泳ぎます oyogimasu

swimsuit 水着 mizugi

symbol (keyboard) 記号 kigoo

synagogue ユダヤ教会 yudaya
kyookai

T

table テーブル teeburu

tablet (medicine) 錠 joo

take v (medicine) 飲みます nomimasu

take away [BE] テークアウト teeku auto

tampon タンポン tanpon

taste v 味がします aji ga shimasu

taxi タクシー takushii

tea お茶 ocha

team チーム chiimu

teahouse 喫茶店 kissaten

teaspoon 茶匙 chasaji

telephone 電話 denwa

temple (religious) お寺 otera; ~ accommodation 宿坊 shukuboo

temporary 一時的 ichijiteki

tennis テニス tenisu

tent テント tento

tent peg テント用ペグ tento yoo pegu

tent pole テントの支柱 tento no shichuu

terminal (airport) ターミナル taaminaru

terracotta テラコッタ terakotta

terrible ひどい hidoi

text v (send a message) メールを送ります meeru o okurimasu; ~ n (message) メール meeru

thank v 感謝します kansha shimasu

thank you ありがとう arigatoo

thank you (for food) ごちそうさまでした gochisoo sama deshita

that あれ are

theater 劇場 gekijoo

theft 盗難 toonan

there そこ soko

thief 泥棒 doroboo

thigh 腿 momo

thirsty 喉が渇きました nodo ga kawaki mashita

this これ kore

throat 喉 nodo

ticket 切符 kippu

ticket office 切符売り場 kippu uriba

tie (clothing) ネクタイ nekutai

time 時間 jikan

timetable [BE] 時刻表 jikokuhyoo

tire タイヤ taiya

tired 疲れました tsukare mashita

tissue ティッシュペーパー tisshu peepaa

tobacconist 煙草屋 tabakoya

today 今日 kyoo

toe 足指 ashi yubi

toenail 足の爪 ashi no tsume

toilet [BE] 化粧室 keshooshitsu

toilet paper トイレットペーパ
ー toiretto peepaa

tomorrow あした ashita

tongue 舌 shita

tonight 今晩 konban

too …過ぎます …sugimasu

tooth 歯 ha

toothpaste 歯磨き粉
hamigakiko

total (amount) 合計 gookee

tough (food) 硬い katai

tourist 観光客 kankookyaku

tourist information office 観
光案内所 kankoo annaijo

tour ツアー tsuaa

tow truck レッカー車
rekkaasha

towel タオル taoru

tower 塔 too

town 町 machi

town hall 市役所 shiyakusho

town map 市街地図 shigai
chizu

town square 町の広場 machi
no hiroba

toy 玩具 omocha

toy store 玩具屋 omochaya

track (train) 路線 rosen

traditional 伝統的 dentooteki

traffic light 信号 shingoo

trail 道 michi

trail map ハイキングコース案
内 haikingu koosu annai

train 列車 ressha; (commuter
train) 電車 densha

train station 駅 eki

transfer v (change trains/
flights) 乗り換えます norikae
masu; ~ v (money) 送金しま
す sookin shimasu

translate v 翻訳します hon-
yaku shimasu

trash ゴミ gomi

travel agency 旅行代理店
ryokoo dairiten

travel sickness 乗物酔い
norimono yoi

traveler's check トラベラーズ
チェック toraberaazu chekku

traveller's cheque [BE] トラベ
ラーズチェック toraberaazu
chekku

tree 木 ki

trim v (hair) そろえます
soroemasu

trip 旅行 ryokoo

trolley [BE] カート kaato

trousers [BE] ズボン zubon

T-shirt Tシャツ tii shatsu

turn off (lights) 消します
keshimasu

turn on (lights) つけます
tsukemasu

TV テレビ terebi

type v タイプします taipu
shimasu

tyre [BE] タイヤ taiya

U

United Kingdom (U.K.) イギリス igirisu

United States (U.S.) アメリカ amerika

ugly みにくい minikui

umbrella 傘 kasa

unattended 無人の mujinno

unconscious 意識不明の ishiki fumeeno

underground [BE] 地下鉄 chikatetsu

underground station [BE] 地下鉄の駅 chikatetsu no eki

underpants [BE] パンツ pantsu

understand v 分かります wakari masu

underwear 下着 shitagi

university 大学 daigaku

unleaded (gas) 無鉛 muen

upper 上の ueno

urgent 緊急 kinkyuu

use v 使います / 利用します tsukai masu/riyoo shimasu

username ユーザー名 yuuzaa mee

utensil 器具 kigu

V

vacancy 空き室 akishitsu

vacation 休暇 kyuuka

vaccination 予防接種 yoboo sesshu

vacuum cleaner 電気掃除機 denki soojiki

vagina 膣 chitsu

vaginal infection 膣炎 chitsuen

valid 有効 yuukoo

valley 谷間 tanima

valuable 貴重な kichoona

value 値段 nedan

vegetarian ベジタリアン bejitarian

vehicle registration 自動車登録証 jidoosha toorokushoo

viewpoint [BE] 展望台 tenboodai

village 村 mura

vineyard ぶどう園 budooen

visa ビザ biza

visit v 訪れます otozure masu

visiting hours 開館時間 kaikan jikan

visually impaired 視覚障害者 shikaku shoogaisha

vitamin ビタミン bitamin

V-neck ブイネック bui nekku

volleyball game バレーボール試合 bareebooru shiai

vomit v 吐きます hakimasu

W

wait v 待ちます machimasu; ~n 待ち時間 machi jikan

waiter ウェーター ueetaa

waiting room 待合室 machiaishitsu

waitress ウェートレス ueetoresu

wake v 起こします okoshi masu

wake-up call モーニングコール mooningu kooru

walk v 歩きます aruki masu; ~ n 散歩 sanpo

walking route 散歩道 sanpomichi

wall clock 柱時計 hashira dokee

wallet 財布 saifu

warm v (something) 暖めます atatame masu; ~ adj (temperature) 暖かい atatakai

washing machine 洗濯機 sentakuki

watch 腕時計 ude dokee

water 水 mizu

water skis 水上スキー suijoo sukii

waterfall 滝 taki

weather 天気 tenki

week 週 shuu

weekend 週末 shuumatsu

weekly 毎週 maishuu

welcome v 歓迎します kangee shimasu

well-rested よく休みました yoku yasumi mashita

west 西 nishi

what 何 nani

wheelchair 車椅子 kuruma isu

wheelchair ramp 車椅子用スロープ kuruma isu yoo suroopu

when いつ itsu

where どこ doko

white 白い shiroi

who 誰 dare

widowed 夫と死別した otto to shibetsu shita

wife (one's own) 家内 kanai; (someone else's) 奥さん okusan

window 窓 mado; ~ (on flight) 窓側 madogawa; by the ~ 窓際 madogiwa

wine list ワインリスト wain risuto

winter 冬 fuyu

wireless internet ワイアレスインターネット waiaresu intaanetto

wireless internet service ワイアレスインターネット サービス waiaresu intaanetto saabisu

wireless phone 携帯電話 keetai denwa

with (attached) …付き tsuki; (included) … 込み komi

withdraw v 引き出します hikidashi masu

withdrawal (bank) 引き出し hikidashi

without 無しで nashide

woman 女性 josee

wool ウール uuru
work v 働きます hataraki masu
wrap v (a package) 包みます
  tsutsumi masu
wrist 手首 tekubi
write v 書きます kaki masu

Y

year 年 toshi
yellow 黄色 kiiro
yen 円 en

yes はい hai
yesterday 昨日 kinoo
young 若い wakai
you're welcome どういたしまし
  て doo itashi mashite
youth hostel ユースホステル
  yuusu hosuteru

Z

zero ゼロ / 零 zero/ree
zoo 動物園 doobutsuen

JAPANESE–ENGLISH

A

aakeedo アーケード arcade

abunai 危ない dangerous

adaputa アダプタ adapter

afutaa sheebu アフターシェーブ aftershave

agemasu あげます v give

ago 顎 jaw

ai 愛 love

aida 間 during

aimasu 合います fit (clothing)

airon アイロン iron

airon o kakemasu アイロンをかけます v iron (clothing)

airurando アイルランド Ireland

airurando jin アイルランド人 Irish

aisu hokkee アイスホッケー ice hockey

aiteimasu 空いています free (available)

aiteiru 開いている adj open

aji ga shimasu 味がします v taste

aji ga usui 味が薄い bland

ajia no アジアの Asian

akai 赤い red

akachan 赤ちゃん baby

akari 明かり light (overhead)

akemasu 開けます v open

akishitsu 空き室 vacancy

akusesarii アクセサリー accessories

akusesu shimasu アクセスします v access (Internet)

amai 甘い sweet (taste)

ame 雨 rain

ameno 雨の rainy

amerika no アメリカの American

amerika アメリカ United States (U.S.)

ane 姉 sister (my older)

ani 兄 brother (my older)

annai 案内 information (phone)

anshoo bangoo 暗証番号 personal identification number (PIN)

anzen 安全 safe (protected)

are あれ that

arerugii hannoo アレルギー反応 allergic reaction

arerugii アレルギー allergic

arigatoo ありがとう thank you

arimasu あります v have

aroma serapii アロマセラピー aromatherapy

aruki masu 歩きます v walk

arumi hoiru アルミホイル aluminum foil

asa 朝 morning

asa 麻 linen

asetaminoofen アセタミノーフェン paracetamol [BE]

ashi no tsume 足の爪 toenail

ashi 脚 leg

ashi 足 foot

ashikubi 足首 ankle

ashita あした tomorrow

atama 頭 head (body part)

atarashii 新しい fresh

atatakai 暖かい adj warm (temperature)

atatame masu 暖めます v warm (something)

ato 後 after

atode あとで later

atorakushon アトラクション attraction (place)

atsui 暑い hot (temperature)

azukemasu 預けます v deposit (money); check (luggage)

B

baa バー bar (place)

baggu バッグ bag

baiten 売店 gift shop

bakkin 罰金 fine (fee)

baree バレエ ballet

bareebooru no shiai バレーボールの試合 volleyball game

baria furii setsubi バリアフリー設備 disabled accessible [BE]

basho 場所 n place

basu バス bus

basu no kippu バスの切符 bus ticket

basu ryokoo バス旅行 bus tour

basu taaminaru バスターミナル bus station

basu teeryuujo バス停留所 bus stop

basuketto booru バスケットボール basketball

basutee バス停 bus stop

bebii beddo ベビーベッド crib

bebii kaa ベビーカー pushchair [BE]

bebii saakuru ベビーサークル playpen

bebii shittaa ベビーシッター babysitter

beddo ベッド bed

beeju ベージュ beige

bejitarian ベジタリアン vegetarian

bekkyo 別居 separated (marriage)

bengoshi 弁護士 lawyer

benjo 便所 restroom (informal)/toilet [BE] (informal)

benkyoo shimasu 勉強します v study

benpi 便秘 constipated

beruto ベルト belt

biichi ビーチ beach

bijinesu kurasu ビジネス・クラス business class

bijinesu sentaa ビジネス・センター business center
bikini ビキニ bikini
bin 便 flight
bin 瓶 jar
biru ビル building
bitamin ビタミン vitamin
biyooin 美容院 hair salon
biza ビザ visa
boku 僕 I (male, informal)
bonyuu o agemasu 母乳をあげます breastfeed
booi furendo ボーイフレンド boyfriend
bookoo 膀胱 bladder
booru ボール bowl
booshi 帽子 hat
booto ボート rowboat
bubun 部分 portion
budooen ぶどう園 vineyard
buhin 部品 part (for car)
bui nekku ブイネック V-neck
burajaa ブラジャー bra
burausu ブラウス blouse
bureeki ブレーキ brakes (car)
buresuretto ブレスレット bracelet
buriifu ブリーフ briefs
buroochi ブローチ brooch
buruu ブルー blue
butsukarimasu ぶつかります v crash (car)
buutsu ブーツ boots
byooin 病院 hospital
byooki 病気 sick

C

chairo 茶色 brown
chairudo shiito チャイルドシート car seat
chasaji 茶匙 teaspoon
chekku チェック check
chekku auto チェックアウト check-out (hotel)
chekku in チェックイン check-in
chibusa 乳房 breast
chichi 父 father (one's own)
chihoo 地方 local
chiiki 地域 region
chiimu チーム team
chiisai 小さい small
chikai 近い close
chikaku 近く nearby
chikatetsu 地下鉄 subway/underground [BE]
chikatetsu no eki 地下鉄の駅 subway station/underground [BE] station
chitsu 膣 vagina
chitsuen 膣炎 vaginal infection
chizu 地図 n map
choo 腸 intestine
choogoo shimasu 調合します v fill/make up [BE] (a prescription)
chooka 超過 excess
chooshoku 朝食 breakfast
chotto ちょっと little

chuugurai 中ぐらい medium (size)

chuumon shimasu 注文します v order

chuusee senzai 中性洗剤 dishwashing liquid

chuusha shimasu 駐車します v park

chuushajoo 駐車場 parking garage/car park [BE]

chuushoku 昼食 lunch

D

daasu ダース dozen

daburu beddo ダブルベッド double bed

daiamondo ダイアモンド diamond

daidokoro 台所 kitchen

daigaku 大学 university

dainingu ruumu ダイニングルーム dining room

dairiten 代理店 agency

daiseedoo 大聖堂 cathedral

danboo 暖房 heater/heating [BE]

dansu kurabu ダンスクラブ dance club

dare 誰 who

debitto kaado デビットカード debit card

deguchi 出口 exit

dejitaru デジタル digital

dejitaru kamera デジタルカメラ digital camera

dejitaru kamera purinto デジタルカメラプリント digital print

dejitaru shashin デジタル写真 digital photo

dekki chea デッキチェア deck chair

demasu 出ます v leave

denchi 電池 battery

denimu デニム denim

denki soojiki 電気掃除機 vacuum cleaner

denkyuu 電球 lightbulb

densensee 伝染性 contagious

densha 電車 train (commuter)

denshi meeru 電子メール e-mail

denshi meeru adoresu 電子メールアドレス e-mail address

denshi renji 電子レンジ microwave

dentoo 電灯 light (overhead)

dentooteki 伝統的 traditional

denwa 電話 telephone

denwa bangoo 電話番号 phone number

denwa o kakemasu 電話をかけます v dial

denwa shimasu 電話します v phone

deodoranto デオドラント deodorant

depaato デパート department store

derikatessen デリカテッセン delicatessen

dii bui dii DVD DVD

diizeru ディーゼル diesel

do 度 degrees (temperature)

dochira どちら which (polite)

doki 土器 clay pot

doko どこ where

doku 毒 poison

dokushin 独身 single (unmarried)

dono kurai どのくらい how much (quantity)

doo 銅 copper

doo itashi mashite どういたしまして you're welcome

doobutsu 動物 animal

doobutsuen 動物園 zoo

doogu 道具 equipment

dookutsu 洞窟 cave

doomo どうも hi

doomyaku 動脈 artery

...doori …通り …Street

dooro 道路 path

dooro chizu 道路地図 road map

dooryoo 同僚 colleague

dooyatte どうやって how

doozo どうぞ go ahead; please

doozoo 銅像 statue

dorai kuriiningu ten ドライクリーニング店 dry cleaner

dorinku menyuu ドリンクメニュー drink menu

doroboo 泥棒 thief

doru ドル dollar (U.S.)

dotchi どっち which

E

eakon エアコン air conditioning

eaponpu エアポンプ air pump

eega 映画 movie

eegakan 映画館 movie theater

eego 英語 English (language)

eegyoo jikan 営業時間 business hours

eekokujin 英国人 British

eetiiemu キャッシュコーナー ATM

eezu エイズ AIDS

eki 駅 train station/railway station *[BE]*

ekonomii kurasu エコノミークラス economy class

ekusukaashon エクスカーション excursion

en 円 yen

enshi 遠視 far-sighted/long-sighted *[BE]*

erebeetaa エレベーター elevator/lift *[BE]*

esukareetaa エスカレーター escalator

F

faasuto fuudo ファーストフード fast food

faasuto kurasu ファーストクラス first class

fakkusu ファックス fax

fakkusu bangoo ファックス番号 fax number

fakkusu shimasu ファックスします v fax

feesharu フェーシャル facial

ferii フェリー ferry

fiirudo フィールド field (sports)

fooku フォーク fork

fooku myuujikku フォークミュージック folk music

fuirumu フィルム film (camera)

fujinkai 婦人科医 gynecologist

fukaku 深く deeply

fukanabe 深鍋 pot

fukumimasu 含みます v include

fukusayoo 副作用 side effect

fukusoo kitee 服装規定 dress code

fukutsuu 腹痛 stomachache

fuminshoo 不眠症 insomnia

fun 分 minute

funsui 噴水 fountain

furaipan フライパン frying pan

furoba 風呂場 bathroom

furui 古い old (thing)

futsuka yoi 二日酔い hangover

futsuu yokin 普通預金 savings (account)

fuutoo 封筒 envelope

fuyu 冬 winter

G

gaaru furendo ガールフレンド girlfriend

gaido ガイド n guide

gaido bukku ガイドブック guide book

gaikokujin 外国人 foreigner

gake 崖 cliff

gakkiya 楽器屋 music store

gakkoo 学校 school

gakusee 学生 student

gamu ガム chewing gum

garasu ガラス glass (material)

gasorin ガソリン gas/petrol [BE]

gasorin sutando ガソリンスタンド gas station/petrol station [BE]

gasu ガス cooking gas

geemu ゲーム game

geeto ゲート gate (airport)

gei baa ゲイバー gay bar

gei kurabu ゲイクラブ gay club

gekijoo 劇場 theater

genkin 現金 cash

gerende ゲレンデ trail/piste [BE]

gerende chizu ゲレンデ地図 trail/piste [BE] map

geri 下痢 diarrhea

gifuto shoppu ギフトショップ gift shop

gin 銀 silver

ginkoo 銀行 bank

gochisoo sama deshita ご ちそうさまでした thank you (for food)

godengon ご伝言 message

gogo 午後 afternoon/p.m.

gomen kudasai ごめんくださ い bye

gomennasai ごめんなさい sorry

gomi ゴミ trash/rubbish [BE]

gomi bukuro ゴミ袋 garbage bag/rubbish bag [BE]

gookan 強姦 rape

gookee 合計 total (amount)

gorufu toonamento ゴルフト ーナメント golf tournament

gorufujoo ゴルフ場 golf course

goshujin ご主人 husband (someone else's)

gozen 午前 a.m.

guramu グラム gram

gurasu グラス glass (drinking)

guree グレー gray

guriin グリーン green

guruupu グループ group

H

ha 歯 tooth

hagaki 葉書 postcard

haha 母 mother (one's own)

hai はい yes

hai 肺 lung

haicheaa ハイチェアー highchair

haiiro 灰色 gray

haikingu koosu annai ハイ キングコース案内 trail/piste [BE] map

hairimasu 入ります v enter

haisha 歯医者 dentist

haiuee ハイウェー highway

hajime masu 始めます v begin

hakarimasu 測ります v measure (someone)

hakike 吐き気 nauseous

hakimasu 吐きます v vomit

hako 箱 box

hakubutsukan 博物館 museum

hamaki 葉巻 cigar

hamigakiko 歯磨き粉 toothpaste

han jikan 半時間 half hour

han kiro 半キロ half-kilo

hana 花 flower

hana 鼻 nose

hanashimasu 話します v speak

hanbun 半分 half

handi kyappuyoo ハンディ キャップ用 handicapped-accessible

hando baggu ハンドバッグ purse/handbag [BE]

hankagai 繁華街 downtown

hanmaa ハンマー hammer

hansode 半袖 short sleeves

hanzubon 半ズボン shorts

haraimasu 払います v pay

hare 腫れ swelling

hareno 晴れの sunny

hari 鍼 acupuncture

hasami はさみ scissors

hashi 橋 bridge

hashira dokee 柱時計 wall clock

hasshin 発疹 rash

hatarakimasu 働きます v work

hatsuon shimasu 発音します v pronounce

hayai 早い early

hayai 速い fast

hea burashi ヘアブラシ hairbrush

hea doraiyaa ヘアドライヤー hair dryer

hea katto ヘアカット haircut

hea supuree ヘアスプレー hairspray

hea sutairisuto ヘアスタイリスト hairstylist

hea sutairu ヘアスタイル hairstyle

heddofoon ヘッドフォーン headphones

heekan 閉館 closed

heeten 閉店 closed

hen 変 strange

henkoo 変更 change (plan)

hera へら spatula

herumetto ヘルメット helmet

heya 部屋 room

heya no kagi 部屋の鍵 room key

hi o tsukemasu 火をつけます v light (cigarette)

hi 日 day

hi 火 fire

hidari 左 left (direction)

hifu 皮膚 skin

higashi 東 east

hiitaa ヒーター heater/heating [BE]

hiji 肘 elbow

hijoo guchi 非常口 emergency exit

hikidashi 引き出し withdrawal (bank)

hikidashi masu 引き出します v withdraw

hikkimasu 引きます v pull

hikooki 飛行機 airplane

hikui 低い low

hima 暇 free (not busy)

hinketsu no 貧血の anemic

hiruma 昼間 noon/midday [BE]

hitchi haiku shimasu ヒッチハイクします v hitchhike

hitoban ni tsuki 一晩につき per night

hitokire 一切れ slice (of something)

hitori 一人 alone

hitotsu 一つ one

hiyake 日焼け sunburn

hiyakedome kuriimu 日焼け
　止めクリーム sunblock

hiyoke 日除け sunscreen

hiyoo 費用 fee

hiza 膝 knee

hizuke 日付け date (calendar)

hoka no michi 他の道
　alternate route

hoken 保険 insurance

hoken gaisha 保険会社
　insurance company

hoken o kakemasu 保険を掛
　けます v insure

hokenshoo 保険証 insurance
　card

hokkee ホッケー hockey

hokoosha 歩行者 pedestrian

hon 本 book

hone 骨 bone

honmono 本物 real

hon-ya 本屋 bookstore

hon-yaku shimasu 翻訳します
　v translate

honyuubin 哺乳瓶 baby bottle

hooki 箒 broom

hookoo 方向 direction

hoomu ホーム platform

hooseki 宝石 jewelry

hoosekiten 宝石店 jeweler

hootai 包帯 bandage

horikomimasu 彫り込みます
　v engrave

hoshiin desuga 欲しいんです
　が I'd like…

hosuteru ホステル hostel

hoteru ホテル hotel

hozon shimasu 保存します v
　save (on a computer)

hyooji 表示 display

I

i 胃 stomach

ibupurofen イブプロフェン
　ibuprofen

ichiban ii 一番いい best

ichido 一度 once

ichiinichiikan 一日間 for (a
　day)

ichijikan ni tsuki 一時間につ
　き per hour

ichijiteki 一時的 temporary

ichinichi ni tsuki 一日につき
　per day

idoosee 移動性 mobility

ie 家 house

igirisu イギリス United
　Kingdom (U.K.)

igirisujin イギリス人 English

ii 良い good

iichiketto Eチケット e-ticket

iie いいえ no

ike 池 pond

iki 行き bound

iki masu 行きます v go

ikkai 一階 ground floor

ikura いくら how much (money)

ima 今 now

imooto 妹 sister (my younger)

imootosan 妹さん sister
　(someone else's younger)

inakunaru いなくなる missing

inryoosui 飲料水 drinking water

insatsu shimasu 印刷します v print

insurin インスリン insulin

insutanto messeeji インスタント・メッセージ instant message

intaanetto インターネット internet

intaanetto kafe インターネットカフェ internet cafe

intaanetto saabisu インターネットサービス internet service

ippoo tsuukoo 一方通行 one-way street

ireba 入れ歯 denture

iremasu 入れます v insert (on an ATM)

iriguchi 入口 entrance

irimasu 要ります v need

iro 色 color

irui 衣類 clothing

iseki 遺跡 ruins

isha 医者 doctor

ishiki fumeino 意識不明の unconscious

ishitsubutu gakari 遺失物係 lost and found

issho 一緒 together

isshuukan ni tsuki 一週間につき per week

isu 椅子 chair

itai 痛い hurt

itami 痛み pain

itsu いつ when

itteki 一滴 drop (medicine)

iyaringu イヤリング earrings

J

jaketto ジャケット jacket

jazu ジャズ jazz

jazu kurabu ジャズクラブ jazz club

jeru ジェル gel (hair)

jidoo 自動 automatic

jidoosha toorokushoo 自動車登録証 vehicle registration

jiinzu ジーンズ jeans

jikan 時間 hour/time

jiko 事故 accident

jikokuhyoo 時刻表 timetable [BE]

jimaku 字幕 subtitle (movie)

jinja 神社 shrine

jinzoo 腎臓 kidney (body part)

jitensha 自転車 bicycle

jitensha ruuto 自転車ルート bike route

joo 錠 tablet (medicine)

jookyaku 乗客 passenger

joosha shimasu 乗車します v board (train)

josee 女性 woman

jungin 純銀 sterling silver

junyuu shimasu 授乳します v feed (baby)

juuden shimasu 充電します v recharge

juusho 住所 address

K

kaado カード card

kaado de haraimasu カードで払います v charge (credit card)

kaato カート cart/trolley *[BE]*

kaaton カートン carton

kabaa chaaji カバーチャージ cover charge

kado no 角の on the corner

kado o magatta tokoro 角を曲がったところ around (the corner)

kaemasu 替えます v exchange (money)

kaeshimasu 返します v return

kagaku 科学 science

kagi 鍵 key; lock

kagi o kakemasu 鍵をかけます lock up

kago かご basket (grocery store)

kai 階 floor/storey *[BE]*

kaichuu dentoo 懐中電灯 flashlight

kaidan 階段 stairs

kaigan 海岸 beach

kaigi 会議 meeting

kaigijoo 会議場 convention hall

kaigishitsu 会議室 meeting room

kaiin shoo 会員証 membership card

kaikan jikan 開館時間 visiting hours

kaikee 会計 n bill (of sale); cashier

kaikyoo jiin 回教寺院 mosque

kaimasu 買います v buy

kaimono 買い物 shopping

kaimono o shimasu 買い物をします v shop

kajino カジノ casino

kakarimasu かかります v cost

kakekin o haraimasu 掛け金を払います v place (a bet)

kaki masu 書きます v write

kakitome 書留 registered mail

kakunin shimasu 確認します v confirm

kamera カメラ camera

kami 紙 paper

kami 髪 hair

kamisori no ha カミソリの刃 razor blade

kanada カナダ Canada

kanadajin カナダ人 Canadian

kanai 家内 wife (one's own)

kanashii 悲しい sad

kangei shimasu 歓迎します v welcome

kangoshi 看護士 nurse

kankee 関係 relationship

kankin shimasu 換金します v exchange (money)

kankiri 缶切り can opener

kankoo 観光 sightseeing

kankoo annaijo 観光案内所 tourist information office

kankoo tsuaa 観光ツアー sightseeing tour

kankookyaku 観光客 tourist

kansen shita 感染した infected

kansetsu 関節 joint (body part)

kansetsuen 関節炎 arthritis

kansha shimasu 感謝します v thank

kanyuu shimasu 加入します v join

kanzee 関税 duty (tax)

kanzen saabisu 完全サービス full-service

kanzoo 肝臓 liver (body part)

kanzume 缶詰 canned

kao 顔 face

kappu カップ cup

kara ni shimasu 空にします v empty

karafu カラフ carafe

karai 辛い hot (spicy)

karimasu 借ります v rent

karorii カロリー calories

kasa 傘 umbrella

kata 肩 shoulder

katai 硬い tough (food)

katamichi 片道 one-way (ticket)

katee yoohin 家庭用品 household good

katto カット v cut (hair)

kawa 川 river

kawa 皮 leather

kawaii 可愛い cute

kawasereeto 為替レート exchange rate

kaze 風邪 cold (sickness)

kazoku 家族 family

keebajoo 競馬場 racetrack

keebi 警備 security

keeburu kaa ケーブル・カー cable car

keekiya ケーキ屋 pastry shop

keeryoo kappu 計量カップ measuring cup

keeryoo supuun 計量スプーン measuring spoon

keesatsu 警察 police

keesatsu no shoomeesho 警察の証明書 police report

keesu ケース case (amount)

keetai denwa 携帯電話 cell phone/mobile phone [BE]

kekkon shimasu 結婚します v marry

kekkon shiteiru 結婚している married

kemikaru toire ケミカルトイレ chemical toilet

kenkoo 健康 health

kenkoo shokuhinten 健康食品店 health food store

keshi masu 消します turn off (lights)

keshooshitsu 化粧室 restroom/toilet [BE]

ketsuatsu 血圧 blood pressure

ketsueki 血液 blood

ki 木 tree

kichoona 貴重な valuable

kigoo 記号 symbol (keyboard)

kigu 器具 utensil

kii horudaa キーホルダー key ring

kii kaado キーカード

kiiro 黄色 yellow

kikan 期間 period (of time)

kimasu 来ます v come

kin 金 gold

kin-en 禁煙 non-smoking

kinenkan 記念館 memorial (place)

kinko 金庫 safe (thing)

kinkyuu 緊急 emergent

kinniku 筋肉 muscle

kinoo 昨日 yesterday

kinshi shimasu 禁止します v prohibit

kinshi 近視 near-sighted/ short-sighted [BE]

kinu 絹 silk

kinyuu shimasu 記入します v fill out (form)

kinyuu shite kudasai 記入して ください please fill out (form)

kiosuku キオスク newsstand

kippu 切符 ticket

kippu uriba 切符売り場 ticket office

kiree きれい clean; beautiful

kiro(guramu) キロ(グラム) kilogram

kiro(meetoru) キロ(メートル) kilometer

kissaten 喫茶店 café/ teahouse

kisu shimasu キスします v kiss

kita 北 north

kitanai 汚い dirty

kitsuenseki 喫煙席 smoking (area)

kitte 切手 n stamp (postage)

kizu 傷 n cut

kizugusuri 傷薬 antiseptic cream

kodomo 子供 child

kodomoyoo no isu 子供用の 椅子 child's seat

kodomoyoo no menyuu 子 供用のメニュー children's menu

kodomoyoo puuru 子供用プ ール kiddie pool/paddling pool [BE]

koin randorii コインランドリー laundromat/launderette [BE]

koin rokkaa コインロッカー luggage locker

koko ここ here

kokunai no 国内の domestic

kokunaisen 国内線 domestic flight

kokusai 国際 international (airport area)

kokusaisen 国際線 international flight

kokuseki 国籍 nationality

kokyuu shimasu 呼吸します v breathe

...komi ...込み with ... (included)

konban 今晩 tonight

konbanwa 今晩は good evening

konbeyaa beruto コンベヤーベルト conveyor belt

kondishonaa コンディショナー conditioner

kondoomu コンドーム condom

konnichiwa こんにちは hello; good afternoon

konpyuuta コンピュータ computer

konro コンロ stove

konsaato コンサート concert

konsaato hooru コンサートホール concert hall

konsarutanto コンサルタント consultant

konsento コンセント electric outlet

kontakuto renzu コンタクトレンズ contact lens

kontakuto renzu eki コンタクトレンズ液 contact lens solution

konzatsu 混雑 congestion

kooban 交番 police station

karai 辛い spicy

kooen 公園 n park/playground

kooka 硬貨 coin

kookanjo 交換所 exchange (place)

kookuu gaisha 航空会社 airline

kookuubin 航空便 airmail

kookyoo 公共 public

kooreesha 高齢者 senior citizen

koori 氷 ice

kooryoku fuyoo 抗力浮揚 drag lift

koosaten 交差点 intersection

koosee busshitsu 抗生物質 antibiotic

koosha コーシャ kosher

kooshuu denwa 公衆電話 pay phone

koosoku dooro 高速道路 highway/motorway [BE]

koosu コース route

koosui 香水 perfume

kooto コート coat

kopii コピー photocopy

koppu コップ glass (drinking)

kore これ this

koruku sukuryuu コルクスクリュー corkscrew

koshoo 故障 breakdown

kotton コットン cotton

kottooten 骨董店 antiques store

kowaremasu 壊れます v damage

kowareta 壊れた damaged

kozutsumi 小包 package

kubi 首 neck

kuchi 口 mouth

kuchibiru 唇 lip

kujoo 苦情 complaint

kuni bangoo 国番号 country code

kurabu クラブ club

kurai 暗い dark

kurashikku ongaku クラシック音楽 classical music

kurasu クラス class

kurejitto kaado クレジットカード credit card

kuriiningu yoohin クリーニング用品 cleaning supplies

kuroi 黒い black

kuruma 車 car

kuruma isu 車椅子 wheelchair

kuruma isu yoo suroopu 車椅子用スロープ wheelchair ramp

kuruu nekku クルーネック crew neck

kushi 櫛 comb

kusuri 薬 medicine

kutsu 靴 shoes

kutsushita 靴下 sock

kutsuya 靴屋 shoe store

kuukoo 空港 airport

kyabin キャビン cabin

kyakushitsu seesoo saabisu 客室清掃サービス housekeeping services

kyandee キャンデー candy/sweets [BE]

kyanpu kinshi キャンプ禁止 no camping

kyanpu shimasu キャンプします v camp

kyanpujoo キャンプ場 campsite

kyanseru shimasu キャンセルします v cancel

kyasshingu saabisu キャッシング・サービス cash advance

kyasshu kaado キャッシュカード ATM card

kyohi shimasu 拒否します v decline (credit card)

kyoka shimasu 許可します v permit

kyoo 今日 today

kyookai 教会 church

kyori 距離 mileage

kyuuden 宮殿 palace

kyuuka 休暇 vacation/holiday [BE]

kyuushamen 急斜面 steep

kyuukyuusha 救急車 ambulance

kyuumee booto 救命ボート life boat

kyuumee dooi 救命胴衣 life jacket

M

maaketto マーケット market

machi 町 town

machi jikan 待ち時間 *n* wait

machi no hiroba 町の広場 town square

machiaishitsu 待合室 waiting room

machiawasemasu 待ち合わせます *v* meet (someone)

machigai 間違い mistake

machimasu 待ちます *v* wait

mado 窓 window

madogawa 窓側 window (on flight)

madogiwa 窓際 by the window

mae 前 before

maekin 前金 deposit (security)

mago 孫 grandchild

maishuu 毎週 weekly

majimena 真面目な serious

makura 枕 pillow

manikyua マニキュア manicure

manshon マンション apartment

mantan ni shimasu 満タンにします *v* fill up (gasoline)

manyuaru マニュアル manual car

massaaji マッサージ massage

massugu 真っ直ぐ straight

masui 麻酔 anesthesia

maunten baiku マウンテンバイク mountain bike

mayonaka 真夜中 midnight

me 目 eye

meeru o okurimasu メールを送ります *v* text (send a message)

meeru shimasu メールします *v* e-mail

meeru メール *n* text (message)

meesaisho 明細書 itemized bill

meeshi 名刺 business card

megane 眼鏡 glasses

meganeten 眼鏡店 optician

memai ga shimasu めまいがします dizzy

memorii kaado メモリーカード memory card

men 綿 cotton

menyuu メニュー menu

menzee 免税 duty-free

messeeji メッセージ message

mibun shoomee 身分証明 identification

michi ni mayoi mashita 道に迷いました lost

michi 道 trail

midori 緑 green

migi 右 right (direction)

miharashidai 見晴し台 overlook (scenic place)

mihon 見本 specimen

mijikai 短い short

mimasu 見ます *v* see

mimasu 見ます *v* look

mimi 耳 ear

mimi ga kikoenai 耳が聞こえない deaf

mimi no itami 耳の痛み earache

minami 南 south

mini baa ミニバー mini-bar

minikui みにくい ugly

miruku ミルク milk (baby)

miryokuteki 魅力的 attractive

misa ミサ mass (church service)

misemasu 見せます v show

mizu 水 water

mizugi 水着 swimsuit

mizuumi 湖 lake

mochikomemasu 持ち込めます v allowed (on flight)

momo 腿 thigh

mondai 問題 problem

moo ichido iimasu もう一度言います v repeat

moochoo 盲腸 appendix (body part)

moodoo ken 盲導犬 guide dog

moofu 毛布 blanket

mooningu kooru モーニングコール wake-up call

mootaa booto モーターボート motor boat

mopetto モペット moped

moppu モップ mop

mori 森 forest

moshi moshi もしもし hello (on the phone)

motto もっと more

motto chiisai もっと小さい smaller

motto ii もっといい better

motto ookii もっと大きい bigger

motto ookii koe de もっと大きい声で louder

motto sukunai もっと少ない less

motto yasui もっと安い cheaper

motto yukkuri もっとゆっくり slower

muen 無鉛 unleaded (gas)

mujinno 無人の unattended

mukai 向かい opposite

mune 胸 chest (body part)

mune no itami 胸の痛み chest pain

mura 村 village

murasaki 紫 purple

muryoo 無料 free

mushi sasare 虫さされ insect bite

mushi yoke 虫除け insect repellent

mushi 虫 bug

mushiboo 無脂肪 fat free

mushiki 蒸し器 steamer

muusu ムース mousse (hair)

muzukashii 難しい difficult

N

nabe 鍋 saucepan

nagai 長い long

nagashi 流し sink

nagasode 長袖 long sleeves

naifu ナイフ knife

naisen 内線 extension (phone)

naito kurabu ナイトクラブ nightclub

nakushimasu なくします v lose (something)

namae 名前 name

nandemo 何でも anything

nani 何 what

nankoo 軟膏 cream (ointment)

naosemasu 直せます can fix (clothing)

naoshi masu 直します v alter (clothing)/fix

napukin ナプキン napkin

nashide 無しで without

nebukuro 寝袋 sleeping bag

nedan 値段 price/value

neeru fairu ネイルファイル nail file

neeru saron ネイルサロン nail salon

nekkuresu ネックレス necklace

nekutai ネクタイ tie (clothing)

nemuke 眠気 drowsiness

nemurimasu 眠ります v sleep

nenree 年齢 age

nenza 捻挫 sprain

netsu 熱 fever; heat

nihongo 日本語 Japanese (language)

nihonjin 日本人 Japanese (people)

nikuya 肉屋 butcher

nimotsu 荷物 luggage/ baggage [BE]

nimotsu hikikae ken 荷物引換券 luggage ticket

nimotsu hikikaeshoo 荷物引換証 baggage ticket

ningyoo 人形 doll

ninshin 妊娠 pregnant

nishi 西 west

nisshabyoo 日射病 sunstroke

nitsuki につき per

no tame ni のために for

nodo 喉 throat

nodo ga kawaki mashita 喉が渇きました thirsty

nodo no itami 喉の痛み sore throat

nomikomimasu 呑み込みます v swallow

nomimasu 飲みます v drink; take (medicine)

nomimono 飲み物 drink

non arukooru ノンアルコール non-alcoholic

nooka 農家 farm

norikae masu 乗り換えます v transfer (train/flight)

norimono yoi 乗物酔い motion sickness

nugimasu 脱ぎます take off (shoes)

nukimasu 抜きます v extract (tooth)

nusumaremashita 盗まれました robbed

nusumareta 盗まれた stolen

nusumimasu 盗みます v rob

nyuukoku tetsuzuki 入国手続
き passport control

nyuuryoku shimasu 入力しま
す v enter (computer)

nyuutoo futaishoo 乳糖不耐
症 lactose intolerant

O

obaasan おばあさん
grandmother (someone
else's)

ocha お茶 tea

odorimasu 踊ります v dance

odoroku hodono 驚くほどの
stunning

ofisu オフィス office

ofisu awaa オフィスアワー
office hours

ogawa 小川 stream

ohashi おはし chopsticks

ohayoo gozaimasu お早うご
ざいます good morning

oiru オイル oil

oishii おいしい delicious

ojiisan おじいさん grand-
father (someone else's)

oka 丘 hill

okaasan お母さん mother
(some one else's)

okane お金 money

okanjoo お勘定 check
(payment)

okoshimasu 起こします v
wake

okugai puuru 屋外プール
outdoor pool

okuremasu 遅れます v delay

okurimasu 送ります v send
(mail)

okurimono 贈り物 gift

okusan 奥さん wife (someone
else's)

omise kudasai お見せくださ
い v show (me)

omiyage お土産 souvenir

omiyageya お土産屋 souvenir
store

omocha 玩具 toy

omochaya 玩具屋 toy store

omoshiroi 面白い interesting

omutsu o kaemasu おむつを
替えます v change (baby)

omutsu おむつ diaper/nappy
[BE]

onaka ga sukimashita お腹が
すきました hungry

oneesan お姉さん sister
(someone else's older)

onegai shimasu お願いします
please (asking for a favor)

ongaku 音楽 music

onna no ko 女の子 girl

oniisan お兄さん brother
(someone else's older)

onsen 温泉 hot spring; spa

oodekoron オーデコロン
cologne

oofuku 往復 n round-trip/
return [BE]

ookee オーケー OK

ookesutora オーケストラ
orchestra

ookii 大きい large

oosutorariajin オーストラリア
人 Australian

ootobai オートバイ motorcycle

ootomachikku オートマチック
automatic car

opera hausu オペラハウス
opera house

opera オペラ opera

ore 俺 I (male, informal)

oremasu 折れます v break
(tooth)

orenji iro オレンジ色 orange
(color)

orimasu 下ります get off
(train/bus/subway)

oritatami beddo 折り畳みベ
ッド cot

osatsu お札 bill/note [BE]

oshaburi おしゃぶり pacifier/
soother [BE]

oshiete kudasai 教えてくださ
い v show (tell me)

oshimasu 押します v push

oshiri お尻 buttocks

oshirifuki おしりふき baby
wipe

oshiro お城 castle

osoi 遅い late (time)

osoimasu 襲います v mug
(attack)

osoroshii 恐ろしい terrible

osusume desu お薦めです I
recommend...

otera お寺 temple (religious)

otoko no ko 男の子 boy

otoko no hito 男の人 man

otoosan お父さん father
(someone else's)

otooto 弟 brother (my younger)

otootosan 弟さん brother
(someone else's younger)

otozuremasu 訪れます v visit

otsumami おつまみ appetizer

otsuri お釣り change (money)

otto to shibetsu shita 夫と死
別した widowed

owarimasu 終わります v end

oyogimasu 泳ぎます v swim

oyu お湯 hot water

P

paato taimu パートタイム
part-time

pajama パジャマ pajamas

pansuto パンスト pantyhose/
tights [BE]

pantii パンティー briefs
(clothing)

pantsu パンツ underwear/
underpants [BE]

pan-ya パン屋 bakery

pasu waado パスワード
password

pasupooto パスポート
passport
pedikyua ペディキュア
pedicure
peepaa taoru ペーパータオル
paper towel
pen ペン pen
penishirin ペニシリン penicillin
penisu ペニス penis
petiito ペティート petite
pikunikkujoo ピクニック場
picnic area
pinku ピンク pink
piru ピル Pill (birth control)
piza resutoran ピザ・レストラ
ン pizzeria
poketto ポケット pocket
pondo ポンド pound (British
sterling)
pondo ポンド pound (weight)
popyuraa ongaku ポピュラー
音楽 pop music
pun 分 minute
purachina プラチナ platinum
purasu saizu プラス サイズ
plus size
purinto shimasu プリントしま
す v print
puripeedo keetai プリペイド
携帯 prepaid phone
puuru プール pool

R

raifu gaado ライフガード
lifeguard

raitaa ライター lighter
raketto ラケット racket (sports)
randorii saabisu ランドリーサ
ービス laundry service
rappu ラップ plastic wrap/cling
film [BE]
rappu ラップ rap (music)
rasshu ラッシュ rush
ree 零 zero
reenkooto レーンコート
raincoat
reesu レース lace
reeto レート exchange rate
reetooko 冷凍庫 freezer
reezooko 冷蔵庫 refrigerator
regyuraa レギュラー regular
rekkaasha レッカー車 tow
truck
renraku 連絡 connection
(flight)
rentakaa レンタカー rental
car/hire car BE]
renzu レンズ lens
reshiito レシート receipt
ressha 列車 train
ressun レッスン lesson
resutoran レストラン
restaurant
rifuto リフト lift
rifutoken リフト券 lift pass
rikon shimasu 離婚します v
divorce
ringu リング ring
rinsu リンス conditioner
rippa 立派 magnificent

risaikuringu リサイクリング recycling

rittoru リットル liter

riyoo shimasu 利用します v utilize

roguofu shimasu ログオフします log off

roguon shimasu ログオンします log on

rokkaa ロッカー locker

rokkotsu 肋骨 rib (body part)

romanchikku ロマンチック romantic

roofaa ローファー loafers

rooshon ローション lotion

rosen 路線 track (train)

ruumu saabisu ルームサービス room service

ryokan 旅館 inn

ryokoo dairiten 旅行代理店 travel agency

ryokoo 旅行 trip

ryoo 寮 dormitory

ryoogae 両替 currency exchange

ryoogae shimasu 両替します v exchange (money)

ryoogaejo 両替所 currency exchange office

ryoojikan 領事館 consulate

ryookin meetaa 料金メーター parking meter

ryookin 料金 charge (cost)

ryoori shimasu 料理します v cook

ryooshuusho 領収書 receipt

ryukkusakku リュックサック backpack

ryuugakuseeshoo 留学生証 international student card

S

saabisu サービス service (in a restaurant)

saafu boodo サーフボード surfboard

sabaku 砂漠 desert

saifu 財布 purse; wallet

saigo 最後 last

saikuringu サイクリング cycling

sainshimasu サインします v sign

saisho no 最初の first

saizu サイズ size

sakana 魚 fish

sakaya 酒屋 liquor store/off-licence [BE]

sakkaa サッカー soccer

sakkaa geemu サッカーゲーム soccer/football [BE] game

sakujo shimasu 削除します v delete

samui 寒い cold (weather)

sandaru サンダル sandals

sangurasu サングラス sunglasses

sanpo 散歩 n walk

sanpomichi 散歩道 walking route

sanshoo 山頂 peak (of a mountain)

sanso chiryoo 酸素治療 oxygen treatment

sara 皿 plate

sauna サウナ sauna

sayoonara さようなら goodbye

seebyoo 性病 sexually transmitted disease (STD)

seekyuu shimasu 請求します v bill (charge)

seekyuusho 請求書 invoice

seeri 生理 period (menstrual)

seeriyoo napukin 生理用ナプキン sanitary napkin/pad [BE]

seetaa セーター sweater

seiritsuu 生理痛 menstrual cramp

seki 咳 cough

seki 席 seat

sekitsui 脊椎 spine (body part)

sekken 石鹸 soap

seminaa セミナー seminar

sen 線 line (train)

senaka 背中 back (body part)

senchi meetoru センチメートル centimeter

senjooato 戦場跡 battleground

senjoozai 洗浄剤 cleaning product

senmon-i 専門医 specialist (doctor)

senmonka 専門家 expert (skill level)

sennuki 栓抜き bottle opener

senpuuki 扇風機 fan (appliance)

sensui yoogu 潜水用具 diving equipment

sentaku 洗濯 laundry

sentaku shisetsu 洗濯施設 laundry facility

sentakuki 洗濯機 washing machine

senzai 洗剤 detergent

serufu saabisu セルフサービス self-service

sesshi 摂氏 Celsius

setomono 瀬戸物 china

setsuzoku 接続 connection (internet)

setsuzoku o kirimasu 接続を切ります disconnect (computer)

setsuzoku shimasu 接続します v connect (internet)

shanpuu シャンプー shampoo

shashin 写真 photo

shashin satsuee 写真撮影 photography

shatsu シャツ shirt

shawaa シャワー shower

sheebingu kuriimu シェービングクリーム shaving cream

shiai 試合 n match

shibai 芝居 n play (theater)

shichakushitsu 試着室 fitting room

shigai chizu 市街地図 town map

shigai kyokuban 市外局番 area code

shigoto 仕事 business

shihainin 支配人 manager (restaurant, hotel)

shihee 紙幣 n bill (money)/ note [BE]

shii dii CD CD

shiitsu シーツ sheet

shikaku shoogaisha 視覚障害者 visually impaired

shikki 漆器 lacquerware

shimasu します v play

shimemasu 閉めます v close (a shop)

shinbun 新聞 newspaper

shindai 寝台 berth

shindaisha 寝台車 sleeper car

shingoo 信号 traffic light

shinguru beddo シングルベッド single bed

shinguru ruumu シングルルーム single room

shinju 真珠 pearl

shinnyuu shimasu 侵入します break-in (burglary)

shintai shoogaisha 身体障害者 disabled; handicapped

shinzoo 心臓 heart

shinzoobyoo 心臓病 heart condition

shirabemasu 調べます v check (something)

shirasemasu 知らせます v notify

shiroi 白い white

shisnkoku shimasu 申告します v declare

shita 舌 tongue

shitagi 下着 underwear

shitsu 質 quality

shitsumon 質問 question

shitsunai puuru 室内プール indoor pool

shitsuree shimasu 失礼します excuse me (to get past)

shiyakusho 市役所 town hall

shizen hogoku 自然保護区 nature preserve

shizuka 静か quiet

shohoo shimasu 処方します v prescribe

shohoosen 処方箋 prescription

shohoosen nashi 処方箋無し over the counter (medication)

shokki 食器 dish (kitchen)

shokubutsuen 植物園 botanical garden

shokudoo 食堂 dining room

shokuji 食事 meal

shokuryoohin 食料品 produce

shokuryoohinten 食料品店 grocery store

shokusen ki 食洗機 dishwasher

shomeeshimasu 署名します
v sign

shoboosho 消防署 fire
department

shoogo 正午 noon

shoohizee 消費税 sales tax

shoojoo 症状 condition
(medical)

shookai shimasu 紹介します v
introduce

shookeesu ショーケース
display case

shookyo shimasu 消去します
v clear (on an ATM)

shoonikai 小児科医
pediatrician

shooten gai 商店街 shopping
area

shoppingu mooru ショッピング
モール shopping mall

shoshinsha 初心者 novice
(skill level)

shujin 主人 husband (one's
own)

shukketsu shimasu 出血しま
す v bleed

shukuboo 宿坊 temple
accommodation

shukuhaku setsubi 宿泊設備
accommodation

shuppatsu 出発 departure

shusseki shimasu 出席します
v attend

shuu 週 week

shuuji yoogu 習字用具
calligraphy supplies

shuumatsu 週末 weekend

shuuri shimasu 修理します
v repair

shuurikoo 修理工 mechanic

shuurikoojoo 修理工場
garage

sobo 祖母 grandmather (one's
own)

sofu 祖父 grandfather (one's
own)

sofubo 祖父母 grandparents
(one's own)

soko そこ there

sokutatsu 速達 express

sookin shimasu 送金します
v transfer (money)

soonyuu shimasu 挿入します
v insert (on an ATM)

soto 外 outside

...sugimasu …過ぎます too...

sugoi すごい amazing

suihanki 炊飯器 rice cooker

suijoo sukii 水上スキー water
skis

suisen shimasu 推薦します
v recommend

suisen 推薦 recommendation

suishoo 水晶 crystal

sukaafu スカーフ scarf

sukaato スカート skirt

sukidesu 好きです v like

sukii スキー ski

sukii rifuto スキーリフト chair lift

sukoshi 少し little

sukyanaa スキャナー scanner

sumi 炭 charcoal

sumimasen すみません excuse me (apology)

sumimasu 住みます v live

sunakku baa スナックバー snack bar

suniikaa スニーカー sneaker

sunoo boodo スノーボード snowboard

sunookeru yoogu スノーケル用具 snorkeling equipment

supiido ihan スピード違反 speeding

supootsu スポーツ sports

supootsu yoohinten スポーツ用品店 sporting goods store

supuun スプーン spoon

suriipingu baggu スリーピングバッグ sleeping bag

surippa スリッパ slippers

surudoi 鋭い sharp

sushi ya 寿司屋 sushi restaurant

sutaato shimasu スタートします v start (a car)

sutajiamu スタジアム stadium

suteki すてき nice

sutokku ストック poles (skiing)

suuji 数字 number

suupaa スーパー super (fuel)

suupaa スーパー supermarket

suutsu スーツ suit

suutsu keesu スーツケース suitcase

suwarimasu 座ります v sit

suzushii 涼しい cool (temperature)

T

taaminaru ターミナル terminal (airport)

tabako 煙草 cigarette

tabako o suimasu 煙草を吸います v smoke

tabakoya 煙草屋 tobacconist

tabeamasu 食べます v eat

tabemono 食物 food

tachiiri kinshi 立入禁止 no access

tada ただ only

taika tobira 耐火扉 fire door

taipu shimasu タイプします v type

taishoku shita 退職した retired

taiya タイヤ tire/tyre [BE]

taiyoo 太陽 sun

takai 高い expensive; high

taki 滝 waterfall

takibi kinshi 焚火禁止 no fires

takushii タクシー taxi

tanima 谷間 valley

tanjoobi 誕生日 birthday

tanoshii 楽しい happy

tanoshimi 楽しみ pleasure

tanoshimimasu 楽しみます v enjoy

tanpon タンポン tampon

taoru タオル towel

tasuke 助け help

tasukete 助けて help me!

tatemono 建物 building

te 手 hand

teeburu テーブル table

omochikaeri お持ち帰り take-out/take away [BE]

tegami 手紙 letter/post [BE]

tekubi 手首 wrist

tenchoo 店長 manager (shop)

tenimotsu 手荷物 carry-on/hand luggage [BE]

tenimotsu hikiwatashijo 手荷物引渡所 baggage claim

tenisu テニス tennis

tenki 天気 weather

tennai no annai 店内の案内 store directory

tento テント tent

tento no shichuu テントの支柱 tent pole

tento yoo pegu テント用ペグ tent peg

terakotta テラコッタ terracotta

terebi テレビ TV

terehon kaado テレホンカード phone card

tii shatsu Tシャツ T-shirt

tisshu peepaa ティッシュペーパー tissue

tobikomimasu 飛び込みます v dive

todokimasu 届きます v reach

toire トイレ bathroom (toilet)

toire no kyuuingu トイレの吸引具 plunger

toiretto peepaa トイレットペーパー toilet paper

tokoya 床屋 barber

tokubetsuna 特別な extra

tokudai 特大 extra large

tomarimasu 止まります v stop

tomarimasu 泊まります v stay (overnight)

too 塔 tower

toochaku 到着 arrivals (airport)

tooi 遠い far

toojoo ken 搭乗券 boarding pass

toojoo shimasu 搭乗します v board (plane)

tooki 陶器 pottery

toonan 盗難 theft

toonyoobyoo 糖尿病 diabetic

tooza yokin 当座預金 checking account/current account [BE]

tooza yoking kooza 当座預金口座 checking account

toraberaazu chekku トラベラーズチェック traveler's check/traveller's cheque [BE]

toreenaa トレーナー sweatshirt

toreeningu jimu トレーニングジム gym

tori 鳥 bird

torikaemasu 取り替えます v exchange (goods)

torimu トリム trim (hair cut)

toshi 年 year

toshiyori 年寄り old (person)

toshokan 図書館 library

tsuaa ツアー tour

tsugi 次 next

tsukaemasen 使えません doesn't work

tsukaimasu 使います v use

tsukaisute 使い捨て disposable

tsukaisute kamisori 使い捨てカミソリ disposable razor

tsukare mashita 疲れました tired

tsukareta 疲れた exhausted

tsukemasu つけます turn on (lights)

tsukeawase 付け合わせ side dish

tsukimasu 着きます v arrive

tsuki 月 month

tsuki 付き with... (attached)

tsumaranai つまらない boring

tsume 爪 fingernail

tsumemasu 詰めます v pack

tsumemono 詰物 filling (tooth)

tsumetai 冷たい cold (food)

tsuretekimasu 連れてきます v bring

tsutsumimasu 包みます v wrap (a package)

tsuuka 通貨 currency

tsuuro 通路 aisle

tsuurogawa no zaseki 通路側の座席 aisle seat

tsuuyakusha 通訳者 interpreter

tsuzuri o iimasu つづりを言います v spell

U

ude dokee 腕時計 watch

ude 腕 arm

ueetaa ウェーター waiter

ueetoresu ウェートレス waitress

ueno 上の upper

uketorimasu 受け取ります v pick up (something)

uketsuke 受付 reception

umi 海 sea

unten menkyoshoo 運転免許証 driver's license

unten menkyoshoo bangoo 運転免許証番号 driver's license number

unten shimasu 運転します v drive

urimasu 売ります v sell

urin 雨林 rainforest

ushiro 後ろ behind (direction)

utsukushii 美しい beautiful

uuru ウール wool

W

waiaresu intaanetto ワイアレスインターネット wireless internet

waiaresu intaanetto saabisu ワイアレスインターネットサービス wireless internet service

wain risuto ワインリスト wine list

wakai 若い young

wakarimasen 分かりません I don't understand

wakarimasu 分かります v understand

wanpiisu ワンピース dress (piece of clothing)

waribiki 割引 discount

watakushi 私 I (formal)

Y

yakemasu 焼けます v burn

yakisugi 焼き過ぎ overdone

yakkyoku 薬局 pharmacy/chemist [BE]

yakyuu 野球 baseball

yama 山 mountain

yasashii やさしい easy

yasui 安い inexpensive

yatoimasu 雇います v rent/hire [BE]

yoboo sesshu 予防接種 vaccination

yodooshi 夜通し overnight

yohoo 予報 forecast

yoku yasumi mashita よく休みました well-rested

yoofukuya 洋服屋 clothing store

yooi ga dekite iru 用意ができている ready

yooshi 用紙 form (fill-in)

yoru 夜 night

yotee 予定 n schedule

yotee ni iremasu 予定に入れます v schedule

yoyaku madoguchi 予約窓口 reservation desk

yoyaku shimasu 予約します v reserve

yoyaku 予約 appointment; reservation

yubi 指 finger

yubiwa 指輪 ring

yuki no ooi 雪の多い snowy

yukigutsu 雪靴 snowshoe

yukkuri ゆっくり slowly

yurushimasu 許します v excuse

yuubin posuto 郵便ポスト mailbox/postbox [BE]

yuubinkyoku 郵便局 post office

yuuenchi 遊園地 amusement park

yuugata 夕方 evening

yuujin 友人 friend

yuukoo 有効 valid

yuusenken 優先権 right of way

yuusoo shimasu 郵送します
  v mail
yuusu hosuteru ユースホステ
  ル youth hostel
yuuzaa mee ユーザー名
  username

Z

zasshi 雑誌 magazine
zeekan 税関 customs
zeekan shinkokusho 税関申
  告書 customs declaration
  form

zensai 前菜 appetizer/starter
  [BE]
zensoku no 喘息の asthmatic
zero ゼロ zero
zubon ズボン pants/trousers
  [BE]
zutsuu 頭痛 headache
zutsuuyaku 頭痛薬 aspirin